Summary of

Tools of Titans:

The Tactics, Routines, and Habits of Billionaires, Icons, and World-Class Performers

By Tim Ferriss

Key Takeaways & Analysis Included

Written by NinjaReads

NinjaReads

Table of Contents

Preface

Author and speaker Tim Ferriss break down the habits, routines, and rituals of people who have achieved success. The book is broken into three sections: healthy, wealthy, and wise, so the reader is bound to learn life-changing advice. This book gives you a chance to channel some of the greats and to always have them by your side.

FOREWORD

ON THE SHOULDERS OF GIANTS

READ THIS FIRST—HOW TO USE THIS BOOK

There are many similarities in people that have achieved success. As you read this book, it is important to understand this is a recipe book. You can skip over parts that are not relevant or of interest to you. The people that have made it in the world are not perfect. They just knew how to enhance what they were good at.

PART 1: HEALTHY

Amelia Boone

Amelia Boone is an obstacle course racer. She won a lot of championships for some of the toughest races out there, like Tough Mudder. Some of her habits include using gelatin, taking saunas, and eating pop tarts before competitions. An example of people using weaknesses is that her favorite races are ones in cold and rain. She knows some of the best competition will drop out due to the conditions. Amelia is a lawyer and has other hobbies, like singing, outside of racing. Her favorite quote is "Nobody owes you anything."

Rhonda Perciavalle Patrick

Dr. Patrick is a well-known researcher. Some of her results have included the findings on vitamin D's effect on the brain's serotonin. She gave Ferriss the information that wisdom teeth can be used for stem cell research. Dr. Patrick also uses saunas several times a week to enhance endurance. She goes over some of their positive effects. Saunas can increase the ability for wounds to heal and also increase growth hormones. Dr. Patrick talks about the positive effects of stretching for the body as well.

Christopher Sommer

Christopher is a world-renowned gymnast coach and athlete trainer. He has developed a rigorous training program. His advice is to work on whatever weaknesses completely embarrass you to build strength. He also suggests to take building your strength slowly. If you rush, you have a bigger risk of injury. The results will happen almost overnight if you are patient. He gives suggestions for exercise that the non-athlete can do, such as j curls. In order to loosen up tense muscles, a vibrator is a perfect solution.

Gymnast Strong

In this chapter, Ferriss goes over exercises used to get your body to a gymnast's level of strength. QL walks incorporate kettlebells while sitting with your legs in the air. A j curl is a deadlift that is slow and controlled. There is a special way to do dips that enhance your brachialis. Ag walks come highly recommended as well. You balance your arms on the floor and use something your feet can slide on. You lift your hips and try to move across the floor. Pike pulses are lifting your heel while you sit on the ground and stretch your hands out as far as you can towards your feet. The cast wall walk is where you do a handstand and walk your hands and feet towards the floor for one repetition.

Dominic D'Agostino

Dominic is a researcher and athlete. His research involves metabolic therapies. He gives advice on fasting, diets, and alternative therapies to cancer. Specifically, Dominic suggests that a ketogenic diet (known as keto) can increase fat loss, may have anti-cancer effects, gives you better use of oxygen, maintains or increases your strength, and it can help with lyme disease. Ferriss suggests fasting as a technique and for a first-time fast he suggests doing three days. You eat your last meal on Thursday evening. Then for the weekend, you keep yourself busy by walking and drinking water with a bit of lemon and salt in it. He suggests sleeping to help your body do some of the work of fasting. Fasting helps reboot your immune system and can kill precancerous cells. This is important because the statistic is 80 percent of people over forty years old get cancer. Dominic even gives advice for late-stage cancer. You can do a ketogenic diet as a base. Try intermittent fasting: one meal per day in a four-hour window. They also suggest a ketone supplement two to four times a day. Metformin and DCA supplements are also suggested.

Patrick Arnold

Patrick is considered a pioneer in prohormone treatments. He created a designer steroid. For a pre-workout shake, Patrick suggests using keto ingredients with a product called Amino Matrix. It helps give back the energy and performance that keto can sometimes take away. Patrick also uses metformin to ward off precancerous cells. There is some research that says metformin could affect mitochondria, but the benefits seem to outweigh the risks for many doctors who take it.

Joe De Sena

Joe founded the Spartan Death Race. He was working a Wall Street job, which involves a lot of risk but did not give him the basics in life. He decided to do the Iditarod on foot to get back to the basics. After he completed this, he decided to develop a race that would break people. The idea was that your fears could be overcome, and you are so much more than your fears. Some of Joe's advice for life is that you should sweat like you are being chased by the police at least once a day.

Wim "The Iceman" Hof

Wim climbed onto Mount Everest wearing nothing but shoes and shorts. He has broken records for ice bath endurance. He has run full marathons in the desert without any water. Ferriss gives an example of one of Wim's exercises, which includes doing a bunch of push-ups and breathing. He recommends to never try any sort of experimental breathing technique in water as someone almost died trying that. Cold exposure is another therapy used. Jumping in cold water or taking cold baths helps alertness and has been related to mood elevation and fat loss. Wim doesn't have any dietary suggestions; he says he eats pasta and drinks beer. He practices giving people heart-to-heart hugs instead of regular hugs.

Rick Rubin's Barrel Sauna

This chapter gives instructions for a barrel-type sauna that heats up in five to ten minutes. You buy an extra-large stove for a smaller area. Ferriss uses one in his own backyard one to two times a day.

Jason Nemer

Jason decided to call the food industry quits. He decided to become a Yogi and travel the world. He gave up his material items and set out. He ended up being the founder of AcroYoga. His advice to people is to play more. Sometimes we lose the childlike play feeling we had. That is one of the reasons Jason developed AcroYoga. It was a way to integrate mindfulness, a workout, and play into one. Jason also talks about having trust in the world. He feels that if he approaches the world and people with trust, he is treated with kindness. He leaves people with the parting thoughts that you can acquire all kinds of knowledge with yoga, but what is important is applying it to simple everyday situations. That's where the answers truly count.

AcroYoga—Thai and Fly

AcroYoga is a blend of three different disciplines. Yoga, acrobatics, and therapeutics, specifically Thai massage. Ferriss gives advice to which poses to try first. He suggests to practice without inverting anyone in the beginning. When you work with a partner, a good rule is "Tell the person what you want, not what you don't want." This is a good rule in life in general. He then gives instructions and pictures for a few different AcroYoga moves. The hippie twist, foiled leaf and leaf hugger, and gravity boots. Each are accompanied by pictures to help.

Deconstructing Sports and Skills with Questions

Ferriss believes that to progress in life and achieve success, you need to ask the right questions. You can do this with any subject, though, you just replace your subject. He then says to track down mentors and ask away.

Who is good at [SPORT] despite being poorly built for it? Who's good at this who shouldn't be?

Who are the most controversial or unorthodox athletes or trainers in [SPORT]? Why? What do you think of them?

Who are the most impressive lesser-known teachers?

Ferriss also asked questions to a basketball expert. His answers gave Ferriss the knowledge to nail three pointers, which he had never been able to do before. It also improved his bowling score. The two sports are relatable.

Peter Attia

Peter is a medical doctor, has done a lot of endurance training, and is a researcher. He starts with his breakfast and what that involves. He doesn't eat much breakfast and also practices intermittent fasting. His fasting is shooting for eating once a day. He has a ketogenic diet but moves away from it when he craves vegetables and fruits. Peter also is obsessed with watches and race car driving simulators. He drinks synthetic ketones and described his first experience of trying it. He said it tasted like jet fuel, but he drank it anyway and then went on a twenty-mile bike ride. He wears a Dexcom G5 continuous glucose monitor to be able to track his glucose levels twenty-four hours a day. He strives to keep his glucose level at an area under the curve. Peter introduced a glute workout to Ferriss that seems easy at first but is difficult upon several repetitions. There are instructions and pictures of this in the book. There are also several blood tests that Peter recommends to prevent death. The five tests are as follows:

1. APOE Genotype: "This informs my thinking on a person's risk for Alzheimer's disease (AD). The gene is far from causal, meaning, having it does not cause AD, but it increases risk anywhere from a bit to a lot, depending on which variant you have and how many copies you have. For what it's worth, the APOE phenotype (i.e., the actual amount of the lipoprotein in circulation in your body) is more predictive of AD than the gene and is obviously a better marker to track, however, [a test is] not yet commercially available. Stand by, though. I'm working on it."

2. LDL Particle Number via NMR (technology that can count the number of lipoproteins in the blood): "This counts all of the LDL particles, which are the dominant particles that traffic cholesterol in the body, both to and from the heart and to and from the liver.

We know [that] the higher the number of these particles, the greater your risk of cardiovascular disease.

3. Lp(a) via NMR: "The Lp(a) particle is perhaps the most atherogenic particle in the body, and while it's included in the total of LDL particle numbers, I want to know somebody has an elevated Lp(a) particle number, because that, in and of itself, independent of the total LDL particle number, is an enormous predictor of risk. It's something we have to act on, but we do so indirectly. In other words, diet and drugs don't seem to have any effect on that number, so we pull the lever harder on other things. Nearly 10 percent of people have inherited an elevated level of Lp(a), and it is hands down the most common risk for hereditary atherosclerosis. The bad news is that most doctors don't screen for it; the good news is that knowing you have it can

save your life, and a drug (in a class called apo(a) antisense drugs) to treat"

4. OGTT (Oral Glucose Tolerance Test): "In this test, you drink a glucose concoction and then look at insulin and glucose response at 60 minutes and 120 minutes. The one-hour mark is where you may see the early warning signs with elevated glucose levels (or anything over forty to fifty on insulin), which can represent hyperinsulinemia, a harbinger of metabolic problems. In fact, the one-hour insulin response may be the most important metabolic indicator of your propensity to hyperinsulinemia and insulin resistance, even in the presence of normal 'traditional' markers such as HbA1C."

5. IGF-1 (Insulin-like Growth Factor-1): "This is a pretty strong driver of cancer. Diet choices (e.g., ketogenic diet, caloric restriction, intermittent fasting) can help keep IGF-1 levels low, if such a strategy is warranted."

Peter talks about Keto warning signs. The diet is not for everybody. He says that if certain markers are elevated, you should stop doing it or use a variation of it. There is a danger in blood tests. You should never go off a snapshot of a blood test, and you should always be aware of any external factors going on at the time the test is given. Peter then lists some of the diseases to worry about if you are a nonsmoker after forty years of age. There are four: neurodegenerative disease, heart disease, cerebrovascular disease, and cancer. A large part of the population will die from these, so Peter suggests being defensive against them if you want to live longer. He suggests that highly refined sugars and carbohydrates can fuel these diseases, so it is best to stay away.

Peter also does not believe in certain kinds of vitamins. He lists off multivitamins, vitamin C, vitamin K, and vitamins A and E as vitamins you already get enough of in your diet. He criticizes multivitamins saying they give you too much of what you don't need and not enough of what you need. He takes magnesium supplements and calcium carbonate. Magnesium maintains healthy kidneys. His favorite brands for vitamins are Jarrow Formulas and NOW foods.

Peter takes low doses of lithium. He doesn't explain why he personally does it, but there are studies that suggest that low doses of lithium can decrease suicidal ideations and suicide in general. Ferriss also now takes low doses of lithium and suggests it works well with him. Peter was overweight at one point at two hundred pounds. He said he thought of getting bypass surgery. His wife thought he was insane. He went to the clinic for a consultation and he was the thinnest person in the waiting room. The nurse thought he was there for a checkup. He said this put things into perspective.

He gives a tip on working out. Skip the running and weight train. It has much more of a benefit when you become older and your bone density is less. He meditates now and is part of Transcendental Meditation. He suggests a few books that helped him on his path to meditation. *10% Happier* by Dan Harris, *Surely, You're Joking, Mr. Feynman!* By Richard Feynman and *Mistakes Were Made (But Not By Me)* by Carol Tavris and Elliot Aronson. Peter's best purchase under $100 was a date with his daughter. He defines success by his older brother, who is a federal prosecutor and has four children under the age of five. His brother said he understands how to do his job better by being a better father.

Justin Mager

Justin helped Ferriss with a lot of his health experiments. He admires Justin because when he was a guest on a podcast, instead of giving out his information for people to look him up, he said for people to go look at themselves. Justin once again suggests that blood test snapshots do not give a picture of a person.

He says that we are a process, not a moment in time. Optimal health means something different to everyone. He also says that asking your doctor what high cholesterol means is important. You should understand the function of something rather than just thinking it is wrong.

Charles Poliquin

Charles Poliquin is one of the best strength trainers in the world. He has trained elite athletes, Olympians, and America's first woman gold medalist in wrestling. He has more than six hundred publications, and his work has been translated into over two dozen languages. He has also written eight books. Poliquin suggests that just because you exercise doesn't mean you should ever have carbs. You should know your body well enough to know if you need them.

One way to know if you are a man is if you can see every single ab. Poliquin describes this as a penis skin over your abs. He says a good strength coach should be able to get a woman to do twelve chin-ups in twelve weeks. His breakfast includes meats, nuts, and eggs. He also says that you should always get more than one opinion with blood tests. For stretch marks and loose skin, he suggests Gaia Herbs Gotu Kola. You have to take them for six months before you see results, but they will work.

Poliquin suggests several blood tests to get every eight weeks:

Morning insulin, morning glucose, reactive insulin tests, and HBa1c. On good doctors, Poliquin feels that the more time they spend with you initially, the better doctor they are. If you need to increase your testosterone, one way to do it is to decrease cortisol. Poliquin says the front squat is the most effective squat. You cannot cheat at this one. Some of Poliquin's favorite books are: *59 Seconds:*

Change Your Life in Under a Minute by Richard Wiseman (for stress reduction), *The 4-Hour Workweek*, and *The ONE Thing: The Surprisingly Simple Truth Behind Extraordinary Results* by Gary Keller. One of the best gifts he ever received was a Bamboo Bench. And the person he thinks of when he hears the word successful is Winston Churchill.

The Slow-Carb Diet® Cheat Sheet

People have lost a lot of weight on this diet. The rules are as follows:

1. Do not eat any white starchy carbohydrates
2. Eat the same meals over and over again, especially for breakfast and lunch
3. Don't drink calories
4. Don't eat fruit
5. Measure your progress in body fat not pounds.

Rule six is take a day to eat whatever you want. Research shows that holding back can be harmful to the body.

My 6-Piece Gym in a Bag

Ferriss brings six items wherever he goes. One is voodoo floss, which is a bandage used to wrap or compress injured body parts, two is furniture sliders, three is a rumble roller, and four is a bed of needles. It is essentially an acupressure treatment that was effective in treating his back pain. Tera's Whey Goat Protein is five, which is great for lactose intolerant people. And six are mini parallettes. These are used in gymnastics and cross fit. This is a version small enough to pack in your suitcase.

Pavel Tsatsouline

Pavel is the chairman of an organization called Strongfirst, Inc. He is a well-known trainer to Soviet and United States special forces. He is the author of a popular book on kettlebell called *Kettlebell: Simple and Sinister*. Ferriss talks about a funny moment he had with Pavel on his podcast, signifying that he has a great sense of humor. Pavel recommends a few different exercises for strengthening. For warm-ups he suggests Halos and a Cossack Squat. Halos are used with a kettlebell and you circle it around your head. Cossack squats are a certain type of squat used with a kettlebell. There are a few things to know about strength from Pavel. He says that strength is one of the best qualities to have, and it is a skill to be practiced: "lift heavy, not hard," keep your reps five and under to build strength healthily, training should be enjoyed, and you should avoid the burn. He also explains a deadlift exercise with low impact that is designed to build your strength. You can find this explained in more detail in his book *The 4-Hour Body*. An important thing to remember when exercising is to build endurance by breathing. There are some great examples of breathing by Amelia Boone. When she does burpees, she does one burpee, one breath. Then, she slowly increases breath per burpee. You should learn the hollow position to do pull-ups. It's where you tuck your tail in. Pavel says to look at gymnasts on rings. Focusing on your core and grip are keyways to increase strength as well. An exercise to increase core strength is a plank. Pavel also says that one way to get stronger is to take breaks between exercising. Do a few reps throughout the day. This is called greasing your groove. This produces enough lactic acid to build strength over the long run. One of his favorite stretches is called kettlebell windmills. He says to look these up on YouTube. His favorite quote is from *Enter the Dragon*: "Sparta, Rome, the knights of Europe, the samurai . . . worshipped strength. Because it is strength that makes all other values possible." Another one of his favorite quotes is "Calm is contagious." People mimic their leaders, so if their leaders are calm, that behavior will trickle down. A book suggestion from him is *Psych*. It gives advice on how to turn your power on and off.

Laird Hamilton, Gabby Reece & Brian MacKenzie

Laird Hamilton is considered one of the greatest surfers of all time. Gabby Reese is one of the most well-known women athletes, primarily for volleyball. Brian MacKenzie is a founder of a CrossFit program called CrossFit Endurance. Laird was Ferriss' trainer. He had Ferriss do the ninety-minute workout with other people he was training. It includes dumbbells underwater, then an ice bath and sauna. Gabby is given new recruits to break with her workout. Pre-workout Laird made everyone a coffee with superfood creamer. Post-workout he gave everyone a concoction with chaga, turmeric, apple cider vinegar, etc. He softens the blow of the sour with kombucha. With their training program, they have a book club of one nonfiction book per month. Gabby suggests practicing going first in life. What she means is be the first person to smile or be kind. She says a lot of people wait on others for this, and it's important to do it whether you are first or not. Ferriss also says that if you run into assholes all day, you are the asshole. A funny story was that they were the first people to try kiteboarding with French non-restartable kites. This is equivalent to boarding with a quilt and a lunch board. An inspiration of a person is Don Wildman. He did eighty days of snowboarding. He always has a group of younger people around him to energize himself. They all talk about exercising in groups. It helps to motivate you to do group workouts. Gabby goes on to give parenting advice. She treats her children like adults. Being a mother has taught her that it is ok to have imperfections. She also says being around men a lot has taught her to deliver a message without emotion and to stick to it. Gabby also talks about how women are taught to be nice. You should be able to do and believe in things that people don't like and be ok with it. She talked about how she doesn't meet a lot of women who do this. The ones that do often have older brothers. They talk about relationships between a man and a woman. Laird says that respecting a woman is the number one most important thing. Gabby talks about how not mothering a man is important, but yet supporting him. It's important to have the same values. Changing someone means that you might not be in love with the person anymore. So be with someone you already respect.

Both Laird and Gabby say you should work on things you are not good at to progress. People should also remember that what people are giving varies on who they are. Something someone is giving in a relationship might look small to you but is big to them. Humility is what they would give people to beat up former athletes. Gabby says to not be afraid as a woman to be singled out and follow your dreams. Do not hold back is her advice.

Laird says to stop drinking and patent all of your ideas.

James Fadiman

James is an expert researcher on psychedelics. He has worked with Ken Kesey and published a well-respected book called *The Psychedelic's Explorer's Guide*. Fadiman starts out by saying his use of psychedelics cured him from anger that had plagued him for years. There is a note in the beginning mentioning that psychedelics are on the same schedule of heroin, yet the recommended doses that are dangerous are way above what you would ever take. James says that you should use psychedelics under medical supervision. There can be a risk with people that have a history of mental illness in their family. Psychedelics are defined as a substance that can separate you from your ego. Psychedelics have been used for centuries in ceremonies. He doesn't consider MDMA a psychedelic because you do not leave your identity behind. Psychedelics have been found to decrease anxiety and depression in patients. Ferriss talks about a good friend of his and his micro dosing plan. He takes ibogaine in small amounts daily. He uses mushrooms every six to eight weeks and ayahuasca for three to six months, two nights in a row. He makes sure that he doesn't take anything four weeks in advance to ayahuasca. It's important to know that not all psychedelics are good for people. Ferriss says that moderate to high amounts of psychedelics can give him a reboot from all of the anxiety and overwhelmed feeling that goes into life. He goes into different dosing of LSD and how it can affect you. The highest dose is a reboot, but you won't remember anything. This is four hundred or higher of mcgs of LSD or five grams of mushrooms. Four hundred mcg can be transcendental, so you should have a guide. Two hundred mcg can be useful for therapy. One hundred mcg is great for creative problem solving. Anything less is considered micro dosing, which makes you a little bit nicer to everyone and more willing to solve problems that cause depression.

Martin Polanco & Dan Engle

Martin is a medical doctor and a program director at Crossroads Treatment. Crossroads Treatment uses ibogaine and DMT to help people recover from addiction. Dan is a medical doctor in psychiatry. On a billboard Dan would put "just be curious." Dan talks about how flotation tanks are great introductions into psychedelics. They are also legal. Both Dan and Ferriss suggest starting with one-hour floats. The best benefit from them is to do two floats per week. Ferriss says he gets fidgety after an hour, so stick to that. Starting with a few a month is a good way to go. The effects bleed over into your life even if they are not immediately obvious.

Ayahuasca, or the purge as people call it, is a psychedelic experience. People often take it in liquid form. It consists of the vine called ayahuasca, and people who make it often add other components into it. Often it is done in a group setting. It is suggested that you do not do it solo the first time but be wary of who you do it with. It is also highly suggested that you do work prior to the ceremony and after. Ayahuasca can have strong effects, but if you don't do the work, you will not sustain what you have learned during the ceremony. It can be rich in hallucinations and it can also make you puke or have diarrhea. This does not happen in everybody. It reboots your body and can have positive effects that last a lifetime if used correctly.

It can be painful though, so it is best to have someone you love and trust to be there for you while you are doing it. It is not suggested to do it as a "party drug." DMT is used to treat addiction, and Martin breaks the dosage down. It is seen to be effective because it connects you with a divine euphoric feeling. If people catch a glimpse of how divine they are, it is hard to put a needle in your arm. DMT can be taken by smoking it, and it has a fast effect. Ferriss suggests he uses edible plants because if you use too much it can make you nauseous. This is a built-in safety mechanism against addiction. Iboga is also used to treat addiction. This is an African plant and is the least-used recreationally of all the other psychedelics. Ibogaine can cause fatal cardiac effects in about one of three hundred people. It definitely should be used in supervision. Both Dan and Martin agree to use it as a last resort for heroin addicts. Micro dosing has anxiety-decreasing effects without the risk of cardiac failure. There are three phases to ibogaine. One in which you are forced to face your ego and life choices. You cannot escape from this. The second phase is introspection. This is also accompanied with a euphoric feeling. This is where addiction is weaned out of you. The third phase is where you can develop new healthier habits and can last up to several months. Ibogaine is seen to be most effective because it completely bypasses the heroin withdrawal. Ibogaine cannot be used for alcoholism, though, it can be dangerous. There are several book recommendations and websites given in the book.

Kelly Starrett

Kelly is a performance coach. Him and his wife founded the San Francisco CrossFit. He has trained world class athletes and written a *New York Times* bestseller titled *Becoming a Supple Leopard*. Kelly can do standing backflips. He drinks a lot of water and puts a pinch of salt in it. Having low sodium is a risk of death-related causes for marathon runners. He is also a sci-fi fan. For men, a great way to understand if you are getting enough sleep is to have a healthy body with normal hormones. This is a great way to measure your own health if you are a man. Kelly says to do cossack squats and overhead squats. If you can't do five reps of overhead squats after running four hundred meters, you need to work on your form.

Breathing is important, so if you cannot breathe, you need to step back in whatever position. Kelly wears compression socks and suggests the SKINS brand. He stresses the importance of sleep hygiene. You should sleep in an all dark area, no light whatsoever. He says that a soft mattress is what people should use. If you lie down and have to cross your legs, it is not soft enough. A pillow under the legs can help flexion. He uses a pulse oximeter to decide whether his athletes should exercise or not every morning. The Nutriforce Wodpak is a multivitamin he thinks is beneficial. For chronic pain, he believes that using a close cousin of the movement that hurt you can help the pain. For kids, he believes that zero drop shoes are good to use.

Paul Levesque (Triple H)

Paul is a professional wrestler and the executive vice president of talent, live events, and creative at World Wrestling Entertainment. He works out late at night and wakes up at six a.m. He says that kids are more prone to doing what you do than what you say. He has a recipe for a keto frappuccino that includes protein powder, ice, Starbucks coffee, and some macadamia nut oil. To overcome jet lag with all the travel he has to do, he always asks if there is a gym at his hotel. He works out, even if it's for fifteen minutes, and it seems to get rid of the jet lag. Ferriss also said this has worked for him. One of the greatest lessons he learned was preparation is super important. He encountered Floyd Mayweather before he went into the ring, and he was completely laid-back watching television. This struck Levesque, and he said something to Floyd. Floyd said that he didn't need to prepare beforehand because he had done that months before. One other lesson is that if you don't do something well, and don't take time to fix it, then do not do it at all.

Jane McGonigal

Jane is a PhD and works at the Institute for the Future. She has written several *New York Times* best sellers; one is titled *Reality is Broken*. She claims that games can help diminish symptoms of depression and can help you sleep, specifically Tetris. She breaks down the psychology of it. Seeing the blocks fall occupies your visual processing center and blocks whatever you are craving or thinking about. Jane recommends *The King of Kong* and *G4M3RS* for documentaries. *Finite and Infinite Games* by James Carse is one of her favorite books. She also enjoys *Suffering is Optional* by Cheri Huber. Her favorite quotes are about the future and stretching beyond what is possible. She says her motto in life is to push the envelope of what we think is possible. If it seems possible, it isn't interesting to her. She doesn't believe in saying negative things about people.

Adam Gazzaley

Adam received his MD and PhD in neuroscience. He did his postdoctoral training at Berkeley. He currently runs a research lab at the University of California, San Francisco. He is at the forefront of developing therapeutic video games. He says past research that says humans only use 10 percent of their brain could be incorrect. He believes that the brain is much more complex than we can possibly understand. He throws monthly parties where he hones in on the type of booze he serves. Recently, he has been into rye whiskey. One of the shows that inspired him was *Cosmos* by Carl Sagan. Advice for his thirty-year-old self is to be fearless. We only have a short amount of time on this earth, so we have to spend it the best we can.

5 Tools for Faster and Better Sleep

Ferriss has had trouble sleeping all of his life, so here are the top five things he does to decompress at night. If Ferriss has a partner with him, he uses acro basing. If he doesn't, he works on decompressing the spine to sleep. He describes a few exercises to do this, the Teeter EZ-Up Gravity Boots, inversion tables, or the Lynx portable back stretcher. One of the things that people have told him that makes a huge difference in their sleep is a ChiliPad. People have differing body temperatures, and this is a blanket that goes over you when you sleep to adjust those temperatures accordingly. It can be used by two different people at a time. A beverage that helps Ferriss sleep is apple cider vinegar with honey and water, or Yogi Soothing Caramel Bedtime Tea. If the tea doesn't work, adding California poppy extract can add the ingredients needed to sleep. Ferriss practices visual overwriting, which for him means ten minutes of gaming (Tetris) or watching an uplifting episode of television. The series he watches and suggests is *Escape to River Cottage.* For darkness, the Sleep Master Sleep Mask works great. For noise reduction, Mack's silicone ear putty is a good solution. Marcam Dohm DS has a white noise sound reducer that works really well. If you don't want to use that, a fan going in the other direction can work well.

5 Morning Rituals that Help Me Win the Day

Ferriss follows five morning routines. He says that even if you accomplish a few of theses a day it is great. He doesn't always accomplish all of them, but he strives to. Making your bed is really important. It is a simple thing you can do to accomplish a task right away in the morning. And when you go to bed, it is something you have accomplished already in your day. It sets the stage for a productive day. He has a positive affirmation or quote to read as well. Then he meditates for ten or twenty minutes. He does five to ten reps of something every morning. He drinks what he calls a "titanium tea." This includes black tea, dragon well green tea, and turmeric with ginger shavings. He tries to write about things he is grateful for in his journal for five minutes, amongst other writing prompts such as "something great that happened yesterday." An opportunity you have today, or how could I have made yesterday better, are also ones he has used.

Mind Training 101

Ferriss finds out that 80 percent of the people in this book have some sort of meditation practice. He gives examples of who they are and what page you can find their practices on. Meditation helps you to concentrate when it doesn't matter, therefore, when you need to concentrate, you have the room to do so when it does matter. Meditation allows you to not be a victim of your thoughts but to observe. This also helps you to be able to choose your own thoughts. There are many ways to meditate, and Ferriss gives a list of suggestions for people.

1. An app like Headspace or Calm
2. Listen to a guided meditation by Tara Brach or Sam Harris
3. Take a transcendental meditation course (this costs a lot of money)
4. Mantra-based meditation; Ferriss tries the word nature
5. Try one of Chade Meng's suggestions, which will be mentioned later on in the book

Ferriss suggests trying ten minutes a day for seven days a week. On a macro level, meditation can have life-changing effects within a year. From a micro perspective, he says that meditation can have effects for himself about fifteen minutes into the meditation.

Three Tips from a Google Pioneer

Chade Meng worked at Google and ended up writing a course on mindfulness called *Search Inside Yourself*. He gives some advice on people starting out in meditation:

1. Have a buddy: It's the same thing as the gym; it's easier to do something when you have someone there to harass you.
2. Start small: Even if you do three minutes a day, it is better than overdoing it and thinking of it as a chore.
3. Take one breath a day: Even if you take one mindful breath a day, it can make a difference.

One thing Ferriss learned from Meng is the Just Note Gone exercise. It is the practice of noticing something is gone. You can do this with one breath, with a song, with a moment. It helps to notice the absence of pain. Another exercise is practicing loving-kindness. Ferriss suggests that once a day you discreetly wish two people happiness. You don't have to say anything out loud, you just quietly do so. You can also spend three to five minutes a day thinking of people close to you that you wish happiness too. It makes a huge difference in your thinking.

Coach Sommer—The Single Decision

Frustration is part of any process. In order to achieve something great, it will definitely be part of the process. Coach Sommer gave Ferriss the advice to make a single decision for your goal. Stick to it no matter what hardships come along. Hardships will come along. Enjoy the process and your journey. That is the most important part of it, the end results are a short part of the process.

PART 2: WEALTHY

Chris Sacca

An early-stage investor in many companies such as Twitter, Uber, Instagram, and Kickstarter. One of Sacca's ideas was to get away from the city. He bought a cabin outside of Tahoe. He didn't have much money at the time. He invited founders of companies out there. He said he found more time to cultivate what he wanted rather than being distracted all the time. The question he asks is how much of your life is being lived to please others. Sacca also suggests going to higher-level meetings. He started sitting in on higher-level meetings, even when he wasn't invited, and would take notes. He also suggests wearing cowboy shirts. It is now his trademark. His advice for challenges that seem unattainable, such as a marathon, is to think, tonight I will be in my bed. Sacca suggests having a beginner's mind to everything. It allows you to see things you might not see otherwise.

Empathy isn't just good for yourself; it is good for business. As a kid, Sacca had what his mom called sweet and sour summers. One part of the summer was spent tagging along with a lobbyist in D.C., and one part of the summer was spent at a blue-collar job. It taught him that he didn't want to end up at a real job. He suggests that good stories and a strong narrative beat a strong spreadsheet for new businesses. Sacca says to be your weird self. He feels that authenticity is one of the largest things lacking in this day and age.

Marc Andreessen

Andreesen created Mosaic, Netscape, Loudcloud, and early HTML standards. He is now a tech investor. If he could put up a billboard, it would say, "Raise Prices." He thinks that tech start-ups low ball themselves and fail because they get too hungry to survive. Andreesen thinks failure is not a way to pivot. It is a way to figure out what you did wrong and fix it. People seem to fetishize it. To find new ventures, he figures out where the nerds hang out at night. He does something to stress test beliefs by having a red team. This is a team of people that argue with you on your biggest beliefs. It helps you to understand all points of view and stick to your beliefs no matter what. Andreesen doesn't look at the past, he keeps on going forward. He thinks it's good to have strong beliefs but keep them loosely. Things are bound to change. Two rules of success are: "Be so good they can't ignore you" and "Smart people should make things." His diet is a mix of coffee and wine to stay awake. Something important to remember is to not overestimate people on pedestals. They were just like you at one point, and they changed the world. You can change the world too. Andreessen studies opposites as well. He doesn't agree with Warren Buffet's investing skills, but he studies them to understand. The chapter is ended by several quotes by Andreesen.

Arnold Schwarzenegger

Arnold won multiple Mr. Universe titles and was a world-renowned bodybuilder. He went on to Hollywood as an actor and also served as California's governor. A big part of Arnold's thinking was that he wasn't doing what he was doing for any other reason than to win. This helped him stay on track. He was a bricklayer and used his second language often to get better profits on his work. Arnold also uses tactics such as asking an opponent whether or not they are sick or had knee surgery. He said it was a way to get into their psyche and make them paranoid. Arnold made millions of dollars in real estate before he became an actor. He decided in his acting classes that he didn't want to be like a lot of other actors who were barely getting by and taking less than savory roles. His advice is never audition but create a niche or use something unique. Agents told him repeatedly that he would never make it due to his body size. Because he wasn't starving and able to bide his time, he was able to get a role eventually which launched his acting career. He made the most money from the movie *Twins*. He did this by forgoing his salary in the beginning to split the profits. The movie made a ton of money. An important takeaway Ferriss says is to ask yourself if you can forgo a short-term gain for a longer takeaway in the long run. Arnold recommends meditation. He also does transcendental meditation and says it changed his life. When he hears the word successful, he thinks of

Cincinnatus. Cincinnatus was called upon to save Rome. He was a farmer. He went back to farming after he saved Rome, twice.

Derek Sivers

Derek created CD Baby. He has a publishing company WoodEgg and has published several of his own books. Reading *Awaken the Giant* by Tony Robbins changed his life. To be able to thrive in an unknown future, Derek says the best option is the one with the most options. When he hears the word successful, he thinks of waiting to answer. The third person that comes to his mind is the one he wants to focus on. Richard Branson was his answer. For people starting out in their career, he says a way to find more opportunity is to say yes to everything. Derek thinks that you can go at your own pace. He graduated college in half the time by figuring out how to do so. His advice to people who are thirty years old is not to think you can't do everything. And think long term. You can do a lot of things, and you have the time to do so. If you have a business model, keep it simple. Once you have success, you can say no to things unless you really want to do them. If you are too busy, you are out of control in your life. On a billboard, he says he would put, "It won't make you happy." He would put it up in shopping malls. Derek was pushing himself to the limit for a morning bike ride, until he decided not to.

He went at a different pace, saw things he normally wouldn't, and made it two minutes over the usual time. Derek doesn't have a morning routine. He treats life as a series of experiments and follows something Kurt Vonnegut said. Even when things are going wrong, pretend to be what you want to be. Derek wrote a silly email to a customer of his CD business. The one email ramped up his business. It didn't take much time. It's the simple things that can make a difference.

Alexis Ohanian

Alexis is a co-founder of Reddit and Hipmunk. He is now an investor and advisor of over one hundred start-ups. He says, in order to stand apart, give a damn. He gives a lesson of giving a damn in less than fifteen minutes. You can make a notification email that your company sends out with a little humor, or something in it that sets it apart. He thinks that giving a damn is important. Details are important and not a lot of people pay attention to them.

"Productivity" Tricks for the Neurotic, Manic-Depressive, and Crazy (Like Me)

Ferriss takes a moment to describe that even successful people suffer. He starts the chapter with a quote about how if you are baring everything, you know you are on the right path. Vulnerability is good. Then he talks about the challenges he has had. Troubles with waking up because he didn't want to waste his time and other distractions. Then he talks about how there was a period after where he had a lot of successes. He says that he is no different from anyone else. He makes a list every morning of three to five things that he needs to do. The top things. Then he focuses on the one that is the most important. No distractions, no social media, no phone calls. This is how he progresses. It's not a magical formula, it is getting things done and not procrastinating.

Matt Mullenweg

Matt is the lead developer of WordPress. Matt doesn't curse and wrote the code for WordPress in a year with little sleep. He has a calm attitude and Ferriss tries to emulate this in his life. He says to plan for success, a lot of people do not do that. He once lost a $400,000 check. He did end up finding it, but he misplaces things a lot. He recommends a book called *The Tail End* by Tim Urban. It points out that we have already spent the bulk of the time we have with our parents. Most of our life is on the tail end of things, so we should enjoy it. Matt's company is all remote workers. He values people that write with clarity. He recommends the book *Words that Work* by Frank Luntz. Matt once ate 104 chicken nuggets while watching the Super Bowl.

Nicholas McCarthy

Nicholas was born one handed. He is a one-handed, world-renowned pianist. Ferriss asked why he didn't use his other arm at any point, and he answered that he did not want to be a gimmick. He told Ferriss to listen to Franz Lizst and Martha Argerich. He recommends a geranium diffuser to keep energized when at home.

Tony Robbins

Tony is a legendary performance coach. He has worked with Oprah Winfrey and Bill Clinton. Ferriss talks about his history with Tony. He read some of his books in high school, and they inspired him to start his own business. Tony says, "It's a belief: life is always happening for us, not to us." Tony suggests that the reason you are suffering is because you are making it all about yourself. He says suffering comes from three thought patterns: loss, less, and never. Ferriss suggests trying the loving kindness method mentioned earlier. That is how he overcame these thought patterns. Tony says the method of state, story, and strategy can help a person overcome challenges. For example, if you are really tired and sit down to try and solve problems, it will be challenging. You need to do what Tony calls "priming."

Priming can mean working out, good rest, or eating healthy. But this needs to be done before addressing life's larger problems. Sometimes problems are not even problems; you just need to eat better or get more rest. Tony's priming includes taking cold showers and breathing exercises. For one of the exercises, he uses the first three minutes to feel grateful. Then he spends the next three minutes feeling the presence of a higher power. For the final three minutes, he focuses on three things he wants to happen. He imagines them done already. Tony has coached some of the world's best investors. There are some commonalities between them all. They are always looking for the downside. They want to invest with minimal risk and maximum reward. They also believe in asset allocation. You have to spread out your stocks amongst bonds because of volatile markets. The last thing they all have in common is that they are all givers. Ferriss asks a "who would be most punchable question." Tony said Obama was for him. Or at least shakeable.

Casey Neistat

Casey is a filmmaker and YouTuber. One of his major inspirations is World War II. One of his favorite books is *The Second World War* by John Keegan. *The Life and Death of Colonel Blimp* is one of his favorite movies. A documentary by Werner Herzog named *Little Dieter Needs to Fly* is one of his favorite documentaries. Casey suggests that when you need inspiration, follow what angers you. He was angered by a ticket he received for not riding in a bike lane. He made a short film about it that went viral.

Casey went outside of the box with a Nike campaign. Instead of making the usual commercial, he asked to use the money to travel the world and make a commercial called "Make it Count." It was a success. And it was an example of how you can make money work for you. His YouTube subscribers jumped when he began to Vlog. He has a strict work ethic. He works long days and nights. When he hears the word success, he thinks of his grandmother who did what she loved her entire life.

Morgan Spurlock

Morgan made an Oscar-nominated documentary. His idea for *Super Size Me* came from a news story about two obese girls suing McDonalds. McDonalds said they couldn't prove their food wasn't healthy. Morgan decided to see what would happen after 30 days of eating McDonalds. He believes you have to cheer for yourself first. He also believes a good story is more important than cinematography. "WATCHING HIM LIGHT IS LIKE WATCHING A MONKEY FUCK A FOOTBALL."—JAMES CAMERON. This is one of Morgan's favorite quotes. He also gives the advice to not be afraid to show your scars. One of his favorite books is *The Living Gita: The Complete Bhagavad Gita—A Commentary for Modern Readers* by Sri Swami Satchidananda. Some of his favorite documentaries are *The Fog of War, Brother's Keeper* and *Hoop Dreams*.

What My Morning Journal Looks Like

A lot of successful people have journals and some of them have been published. Ferriss is giving an example of his own journal. He uses this quote to inspire him: "Once we get those muddy, maddening, confusing thoughts [nebulous worries, jitters, and preoccupations] on the page, we face our day with clearer eyes." Ferriss stresses that it is important to write for yourself and nothing else. He shares a journal entry from one day. He then analyzes it. He says there are two points. He is trying to figure things out and writing might help. He also thinks that it cages his monkey mind. If you get your problems out, it keeps them from bouncing around in your mind all day. He thinks that complaining on paper can make you more effective throughout your day.

Reid Hoffman

Reid is a tech insider and investor in LinkedIn, Facebook, and QuestBridge. He developed tools to solve problems by playing

Avalon Games and reading Sun Tzu as a boy. He suggests following Ludwig Wittgenstein as a philosopher. Wittgenstein talks about how to use language to your advantage. He asks himself what the easiest problem to solve is, then he solves it. He uses this as a strategy with work. Reid has a method of jotting down a problem before he goes to bed so his subconscious can work on it. He said it is helpful for him. Reid's first principle is speed. He is okay with a mistake rate if you get things done fast.

He thinks the best people to have close to you are those that make suggestions to something you are doing. Reid seeks one big reason to do something, not several little ones.

Peter Thiel

Peter founded PayPal amongst other big tech companies. The advice given from Peter is worth reading a few times. Ferriss suggests reading the suggestions several times. One of the questions

Ferriss asks is what Peter would do if he could go back twenty-five years. Peter said he wouldn't wait. He asks the question, what are my ten-year goals? What could I do to make them happen in six months? He said don't wait on ideas. Make them happen. Peter thinks failure in business happens for more than one reason. It's a good thing to delve into so you don't make the same mistakes twice. Ferriss asks Peter what he thinks the biggest tech trends are in the future.

Peter stresses to not think about current trends but to make up your own idea. None of the big trends will be from something that has already happened. Although Peter went to Stanford, he stresses that people don't need a fancy education to succeed. He thinks people from all walks of life should have ideas to keep it diverse. He is in favor of learning but not as credentials as a means of education. He thinks people should look for motivation to learn, rather than to earn a fancy education. If he could change one thing about himself, he says that he would be less competitive.

You lose out on being good at important things if you just focus on one thing. Peter also thinks we shouldn't mistake conventions with truth. The two do not always equate. Peter often says, "Tell me something that is true that people often disagree with you on." Ferriss shares three of seven questions Peter would ask someone starting a business.

The Monopoly Question: Are you starting with a big share of a small market?

The Secret Question: Have you identified a unique opportunity that others don't see?

The Distribution Question: Do you have a way to not just create but deliver your product?

Seth Godin

Seth is the author of a successful blog. He has written over 35 books that cover the subjects of marketing and challenging the status quo. One of his pieces of advice is to be a meaningful specific rather than a wandering generality. A lot of people want things from you. If you want to accomplish your purpose, you will need to learn to say no to a lot of those if it doesn't fit with your mission. Seth says that money is a story. It's good to make a story you are happy with. People with a lot of good ideas have even more bad ideas. Generate a lot of ideas and you will find one good one in there. You can also make up the narrative in your life. It doesn't help you to keep track of all of the times you were wronged or rejected. A better narrative is to keep track of all the times you took a risk and it worked out. Don't retreat into your negative story, which is something Ferriss wrote after healing work.

People spend most of their time dealing with the cards they have been dealt. If you try a different approach, or change the people you are around, you might have a different result. You have more power than you think, and the big task is deciding what to do with it. Another approach to life is the idea of pushing something downhill rather than up. Your idea could have a niche that you haven't identified that needs you, not the other way around.

There's a simple theory in marketing. If you show ten people an idea, and they think it's good and share it, then you are on your way. If they don't, you are not on your way. Also, pick a small project. Start small, that can lead to something big. He says that nobody gets a Suzuki tattoo. They get Harley tattoos. You can build something aspirational. Seth suggests to ignore quantifying things. He says to put good things out in the world and ignore all the racket. In raising kids, he says to give them attention and take time away from screens. He also says two important things in raising children is to urge them to think about leading and solving problems. His logic is that people besides us will always be willing to work harder as cogs.

Seth thinks that people are flexible as well, that you grow. You are not made from birth. Anybody can change. There are several audiobooks that Seth likes: *Goals: Setting and Achieving Them on Schedule, How to Stay Motivated,* and *Secrets of Closing the Sale* by Zig Ziglar; works by Pema Chödrön; *Leap First* by Seth Godin; *The Art of Possibility* by Rosamund Stone Zander and Benjamin Zander; *The War of Art* by Steven Pressfield; *Just Kids* by Patti Smith ("this is the single best audiobook ever recorded by Patti Smith"); and *Debt* by David Graebel. Seth's best purchase of one hundred dollars or less is chocolate. The advice he would give to his thirty-year-old self is no advice. He had a lot of bumps, but without those bumps, he wouldn't be who he is. One quirk of his is that he makes coffee vodka even though he doesn't drink coffee or vodka.

James Altucher

James is a hedge fund manager. He has started twenty businesses. Seventeen failed and three made him a lot of money. He wrote the book *The Power of No*. James says if you can't come up with ten ideas than generate twenty. Sometimes trying to be perfect gets in the way of finding a great idea. He gives ideas on his lists, which he recommends writing every morning. Some of the lists include ten businesses where you can get rid of the middleman, and ten ways to solve a problem with the IRS. It is okay to have selective ignorance. James realized this after working at a newspaper.

All they wanted to focus on was bad news. He doesn't think people need to explain why they say no to things. And if people are stuck trying to find a single purpose, don't. People don't need one single purpose to be happy in life.

How to Create a Real-World MBA

Ferriss explains some tactics to avoid the cost of school while gaining experience to help you learn about the world of business. Start by having lunch with people who can help you in whatever expertise you are trying to learn. Plan to lose a certain amount of money to get where you need to go. He thinks you should have insider access if you are investing in startups. You should be comfortable losing money. You should have managed a business in the past if you plan to be successful in investing. And you should only invest 10 to 15 percent of your liquid funds. Make rules for yourself so you can track patterns. Here are some of Ferriss' rules:

- If it has a single founder, the founder must be technical. Two technical co-founders are ideal.
- I must be eager to use the product myself. This rules out many great companies, but I want a verified market I understand.
- Related to the previous point: consumer-facing product or service (e.g., Uber, Twitter, Facebook, etc.) or small-business focused

product or service (e.g., Shopify), not big enterprise software. These are companies whose valuations I can directly impact through my platform, promotion to my audience, introductions to journalists, etc.

- More than one hundred thousand active users OR serial founder(s) with past exits OR more than ten thousand paying customers. Whenever possible, I want to pour gasoline on the fire, not start the fire.
- More than 10 percent month-on-month activity growth.
- Clean "cap table," minimal previous financing (or none), no bridge rounds.
- U.S.-based companies or companies willing to create U.S.-based investable entities. Shopify started in Canada, for instance.
- Have the founders ever had crappy service jobs? If they have, they will be more grounded. He stresses to follow your rules.

Ferriss says sometimes an exit is the best plan you can have.

He thinks being an adviser is a great way to learn investing. Doing both is the way to go. Diversifying is always a good plan, he says. He breaks down the price of degrees and how you can invest to get the same quality of education without the cost.

Scott Adams

Scott is the creator of Dilbert. He has written other bestselling novels as well. Scott's mother gave birth to him under hypnosis and felt no pain. A blog post of his titled "The Day You Become a Better Writer" has influenced a lot of people. *F Minus* and *Pearls Before Swine* are two comics he suggests. There are six elements of humor according to Scott. Naughty, clever, cute, bizarre, mean, and recognizable. He thinks you need two to succeed. He gives an example of an animal talking and behaving like a human. Bizarre and recognizable. He thinks sometimes it's ok to sleep on ideas when in doubt. Scott dives into how he says systems rather than goals. Systems are projects you take on and start meeting people along with doing things. He uses the example of a blog. His blog didn't generate income, but it opened a lot of doors for him, which led to income later down the line. Ferriss also had a similar experience with his podcast. Affirmations was something Scott discovered when he was younger training to be a hypnotist. He said if you say an affirmation fifteen times a day, things will happen for you. He also predicted Trump becoming president a year before it happened. He believed that Trump had hypnotist powers as well as media savvy.

He finds material by listening to his body more than his mind. If he reads something in the morning that gives him a rush of anger or emotion, he knows it's good. Ferriss asked him how he reduces his stress. He does so by having diversification. He has several different jobs, sources of money, etc. This helps eliminate stress. His logic to be successful is as follows: "If you want to be average, it doesn't take much planning. Just stay out of trouble, go to school, and apply for jobs you might like. But if you want something extraordinary, you have two paths:

1. Become the best at one specific thing.
2. Become very good (top 25 percent) at two or more things.

Shaun White

Shaun White is a professional snowboarder and skateboarder. He has won two Olympic medals. He was born with a heart defect and had many surgeries because of it. Before an Olympic event, his self-talk is, I'm going to do the best I can. At the end of the day, I can go home to my family. He overcame peer pressure at an event by sticking to his goals. He rode at an event where he paid his way, and the rest of the people wanted to split the winning pot. They all had their way paid. Shaun refused to split the money and won the event. When he sets goals, he sets a big one, like winning the Olympics. He also sets a ridiculous one, like wearing American Flag pants when he wins. Growing up in Southern California ended up being an asset to Shaun. He was able to snowboard at a park that had less people and amazing jumps. Shaun trained to play guitar. He formed a band with some friends. They were invited to play at Lollapalooza but at the kids' stage. Another band didn't show up, and he got to play the main stage. He gifts people *Fifty Shades of Chicken*.

The Law of Category

Ferriss talks about how if you cannot be the best at creating something new, find a category to improve something that exists. An example of this is how Miller Lite created a lite domestic beer after Amherst Lite. He says as well to create the language of an idea or trend. He coined the term "lifestyle design" with his book.

Chase Jarvis

Chase Jarvis is a world class photographer. He started when he was younger. He took pictures of his friends skiing and snowboarding. They were using equipment and new gear, so he got paid to take pictures for those companies. He says that he charged a lot of money for his first gig. He had the experience at that point. Chase and Ferriss say you should hone your craft before giving into advertisement money. He says that the more audience you have, the better deals you will have. Chase also says you should amplify your strengths rather than focus on your weaknesses. Specialization is for insects, meaning that humans can do almost anything, so try a lot of different things and they will bleed into one another.

Dan Carlin

Dan created the popular podcast *Hardcore History*. Dan's advice is to not be worried about whether you are qualified at something or not. He was not qualified at history, but he could tell stories. He was urged to tell his stories on a podcast, and he couldn't find a reason not to. He also says to play on your strengths. He talks really loudly so he has people introduce him that way. His advice for his thirty-year-old self would be not to worry. But all that worry may not have gotten him where he is, so he takes that back.

Ramit Sethi

Ramit graduated from Stanford with several bachelors and master's degrees. He built a personal finance blog that went from a student project to a successful company. Ramit gains almost all of his business through email. Ferriss tried the same and his business grew. Some of the software he uses is Infusionsoft and Visual Website Optimizer. Ramit says, "Tactics are great, but tactics are commoditized. One of the books he gives away the most is *Age of Propaganda* by Anthony Pratkanis. He studies behavioral psychology to understand the power of persuasion. There is an article by Kevin Kelly called "1,000 True Fans." The advice is that if you can build one thousand fans, you can work upward from there. It motivated Ramit to produce meaningful content. It was the same with Ferriss. They also both recommend to give most of your stuff away for free, then to charge really high for some content. Ferriss also uses the contacts he has for finding out about investments. Ramit is obsessed with checklists. He loves a book called *The Checklist Manifesto* Atul Gawande. One of his heroes is a guy named Mark Bustos. He is a famous hairstylist in New York City. On weekends, he cuts the hair of homeless people and records their stories. Jay Abraham, who wrote *Getting Everything You Can Out of All You've Got* is one of Ramit's favorite authors. In India, people are really blunt and will tell you if you are fat.

1,000 True Fans—Revisited

Kevin Kelly breaks down 1,000 True Fans. He says that if you can get on thousand true fans, it can generate enough income for you to live a decent lifestyle. It can also lead to bigger things. But shooting for on thousand fans is much more doable. A true fan is someone that will buy anything you do. If they spend $100 a year, then you will make $100,000 a year. You have to have a direct relationship with your fans to do this. The internet has allowed people to find whatever desire they have. It also makes it possible for the artist to have a direct relationship with the person. There are several platforms to use for funding. Kickstarter and Patreon are two. They have different mechanisms on how they work. It may work differently for different artists. You can adjust accordingly for what you need. Ferriss offers a worksheet to figure out what income you want.

Hacking Kickstarter

Ferriss gives instructions on how to hack $100,000 in Kickstarter in 10 days. He uses Mike Del Ponte for pointers. Mike did raise this amount for the start-up for Soma. Keep in mind that VA means virtual assistant. Mike finds his VA on Upwork or Zirtual. If you have an idea for a product, launching it can be risky. Crowdfunding platforms like Kickstarter and Indiegogo make it possible to launch a product before it goes to manufacturing. This gauges the popularity of a product, and it can help raise thousands of dollars. Also, it brings to light if a product is not popular.

Mike interviewed some of the top earners on Kickstarter, hired a VA, and used principles from Ferriss' book to start his campaign. First, Mike applies the Minimum Effective Dose (MED) principle. His friend Clay Hebert is a Kickstarter expert. He says to use bit.ly tracking. Bit.ly is a link shortening trick. If you add a + to any bit.ly link, you can see the statistics associated with that link. To discover the top referral sites, Mike used his VA to find a list of similar Kickstarter projects. The VA then focused on two things: getting coverage on the right blogs and activating social networks to get coverage. You can find relevant bloggers by searching Google images. The goal will be to find ten similar projects on Kickstarter. Once you find those, find an image from the campaign, and right click on it to save two to three desktop images. Drag those images into your google search bar.

Review the blogs listed on the search bar to see what might be relevant. Fill out the author's information on a media spreadsheet. Now you will have a bunch of relevant blogs. Your VA can find even more by using similar-sites.com. You can research web traffic on alexa.com or similarweb.com. A huge readership is not always the most important thing for blogs, but it is worth knowing. Identifying relationships on Facebook is the next step. It's much easier to get on a blog if you have a mutual connection. See what mutual friends might know the blogger and get introduced that way if possible. You can also use LinkedIn. Using TextExpander or Boomerang will help you save a lot of time typing. You can use Ferriss' book *Four Hour Workweek* for additional tips.

Alex Blumberg

Alex is the founder of Gimlet Media and has produced several award-winning podcasts. He used to produce *This American Life*. Ferriss points out that the reason a podcaster is in the wealthy section is because in order to progress, you need to ask the right question. This is where Alex comes in. Asking the dumb question is often the best way to go. Alex found a lot of success by asking "why are banks loaning money to people who cannot repay it." Some tools for interviewing are that you should never ask yes or no questions. Alex covers setting, emotions, and details. Here are some prompts:

"Tell me about a time when . . ."

"Tell me about the day [or moment or time] when . . ."

"Tell me the story of . . . [how you came to major in X, how you met so-and-so, etc.]"

"Tell me about the day you realized ____ . . ."

"What were the steps that got you to ____?"

"Describe the conversation when . . ."

Some follow-up questions are:

"How did that make you feel?" and "What do you make of that?"

Some general questions are: "

"If the old you could see the new you, what would the new you say?"

"You seem very confident now. Was that always the case?"

"If you had to describe the debate in your head about [X decision or event], how would you describe it?"

Alex uses Audio-Technica AT8035 shotgun microphone, TASCAM DR-100mkII recorder, Sony MDR-7506 headphones, and XLR cables. For software, he uses Avid Pro Tools and Chartbeat for analytics.

The Podcast Gear I Use

Ferriss breaks down the podcast gear he uses. You can find more information about it in his book *The Four-Hour Workweek*. He uses a Zoom six-track portable recorder. This is what he uses for in person interviews along with the Shure SM58-LC microphone. These are commonly used and simple mics. He doesn't use mic stands for people, so they are forced to hold the mic and be more consistent. He says to put batteries in the recorder every time you use. You need an XLR three-pin cord to connect the microphone to the recorder. He suggests six feet in length. A Bluecell five-pack of windscreen foam microphone covers will help shut out extra noise. Ecamm call recorder is what he uses for interviews on Skype. Most of his interviews are on Skype. The Audio-Technica ATR2100-USB cardioid dynamic USB/XLR microphone is what he uses for Skype interviews. He uses the Yellowtec iXm for traveling. For editing, he uses Garageband. He said if you don't keep it simple, you will quit. He records full-length conversations to save time on post-production. Other people use Ableton or Hindenburg.

Ed Catmull

Ed helped found Pixar and is the current president of Walt Disney and Pixar Studios. Ed says we all begin with suck. The first versions of *Toy Story* and *Ratatouille* were horrible. He said he isn't just saying that to be humble; they really were horrible. Ed talks about the negotiation that Steve Jobs had with Pixar and Disney. Steve had an elaborate plan to launch Pixar as a public company. The endgame was to be fifty-fifty with Disney, who was funding their first three films. It hinged on *Toy Story* being a success, and it was. Ed suggests if you have trouble reading to try audiobooks. He did this with *The Iliad*. He realized that was a way he could absorb things because he was bad at focusing while reading. He started to listen to audiobooks while on his commute and learned a lot about several different subjects. Ed initially was going to go to school to be an illustrator but changed to physics. He didn't think he would be good enough to work at Disney. Ed thinks that his education is applicable to be an illustrator because what artists do is learn how to see. You can learn how to see with any subject. He practices Vispassana meditation thirty to sixty minutes a day and most often gifts the book *One Monster After Another* by Mercer Mayer.

Tracy DiNunzio

Tracy is the founder of Tradesly. She has helped countless people build revenue. Her advice is to not complain. She was born with Spinal Spinosa and used to complain about the pain she experienced. Tracy followed some advice from Stephen Hawking. He said, "When you complain, nobody wants to help you." If you spend time thinking of things that are wrong, that is what you will attract. She tried having a complaining diet with other people. Furthermore, she tried to stop her negative thinking. It took a while to stick, but she noticed positive results. She even felt less physical pain. When you start your pitch, Tracy says, you should pick the right audience to suck in front of. Even Jerry Seinfeld picks smaller venues to hone his material. Pick ten people you don't care too much about to pitch to, then when you get better, pick bigger people.

Phil Libin

Phil is the founder of Evernote. Evernote has about 150 million users. When asked who he thinks the most successful person is, he said the iPhone. Phil says a must watch documentary is *The Gatekeepers*. Phil always wanted to go to Mars. He started to plan to go to Mars. He spoke with Elon Musk about what he needed to do. He mentioned to Jeff Bezos his dream of going to Mars, and Jeff said it was a stupid idea. Jeff said the base of the idea is overcoming gravity. Once we do that, it would be better to live in space on space stations than on the rough terrain of Mars. Phil said his mind was blown by this. It made him realize to question assumptions. One person Phil admires is Hiroshi Mitikani. He is the CEO and founder of

Rakuten, which is one of Japan's largest online marketplaces. He taught Phil the ten and three rule. That means that when a company grows in 10s or 3s in size, you usually need to entirely change the way things are done. It is a good idea to reassess your company and see what systems are holding you back.

Chris Young

Chris is a chef and innovator. He wrote *Modernist Cuisine*. Before he was a chef, he had degrees in biochemistry and mathematics. He would put on a billboard, "It all worked out anyway." Chris did not have a great time in high school. He would also say that the interesting jobs are the ones you make up. When Chris was younger, his dad said not to worry about what he was going to do. He told him to learn the things that interest him and become good at them. That will leverage an income for you. The person that

Chris thinks is interesting is a guy named Heston Blumenthal. Heston poses an interesting question to people of every background. He is naturally curious. Chris was asked by investor Gabe Newell what Chris would make for one hundred million dollars. This would be a product nobody else could compete with due to the price of it. Chris got his first job by appealing to chef William Belicki's ego. Chris asked at the end of his internship if he could work full time. William said he didn't have a place for him. Chris asked if he had suggestions for where he could find work. William said he should probably just work for him. Chris thinks that the statement of working for other people struck William's ego; he was the only person Chris could learn from. Chris learned in his first job not to substitute subpar food for what the actual dish was. Quality is of the utmost importance, even if you have to make it different, make it with quality. Chris's father and Winston Churchill are the people he considers successful. He suggests reading *The Second Law*. It has helped Chris to sort out how things and people work.

Daymond John

Daymond is the CEO and founder of FUBU. He started out with a $40 budget and grew his company into a multi-billion-dollar business. Daymond says that the real magic in growing a business is sales. He says if you get out and start producing attention around a product, things will happen. He says that five days a week he says his five goals to himself. Once in the morning and once in the evening. His parents taught him that his homework would make him rich. Not his day job. He threatens that if you play football with him, he will beat you. The best investment he ever made was being a foot messenger in Manhattan. He learned a lot about different types of people. The happiest often weren't the most well paid. He says that "money is a great servant but a horrible master." He suggests the following books: *Think and Grow Rich, Who Moved My Cheese?, Blue Ocean Strategy, Invisible Selling Machine, The Richest Man in Babylon,* and *Genghis Khan and the Making of the Modern World.*

Noah Kagan

Noah is the number thirty employee at Facebook and the number four at Mint.com. He founded the company SumoMe. For people wanting to be entrepreneurs, he suggests taking the coffee challenge. The coffee challenge is ordering a coffee somewhere and asking for 10 percent off. It's a good test on putting yourself out there. He aims to optimize tools that are easy to upgrade. One is a mousepad. You can increase the speed of your mousepad by going into settings, or system preferences, and doubling your current speed. He also suggests investing in the best router you can find. The ASUS RT-AC87U Wireless-AC2400 dual band gigabit router is what Noah uses. He said Lasik is one of the best investments he has made of all time. To make effective use of your time, install Facebook New Feed Eradicator, buy ScheduleOne, and use FollowUp.cc. He uses the + trick in Gmail. All it means is adding a + to your login email when signing up for a new service. He says you shouldn't find time, but you should make time for things that are important. He also recommends the book *Surely, You're Joking, Mr. Feynman!* by Richard P. Feynman. Some of the worst advice he has heard is to grow your social media. Some of the people he has learned from in the past are Andrew Chen (growth team at Uber), Tomasz Tunguz (venture capitalist and software as a service [SaaS] expert), and Jonathan Siegel (chairman of Earth Class Mail). For hiring, he uses the question who instead of what. He recommends *The Gary Halbert Letter* (also *The Boron Letters*) and *Ogilvy on Advertising* for tools on copywriting. His best purchase was a Nutribullet. To motivate himself, he only puts motivating people in his Instagram feed. He gained forty pounds of muscle mass by doing this.

Kaskade

Kaskade is a DJ that is often credited for creating progressive house. He bought his first gear from a gig he got at a local club in Utah. He asked the club owner what the slowest night was, and the owner said Monday. He cut a deal with Kaskade that he could have the night at a discount if he invited his friends in. It became a huge deal over time and that's how he bought his first gear. Kaskade said he always tries to make things like traveling with his family a huge priority. He sits back and thinks about what is most important to him. Then he goes after that. His dad always told him, "Remember who you are." Some of his favorite albums are anything by Kraftwerk and Daft Punk's *Homework*.

Luis von Ahn

Luis is the CEO of Duolingo and is a professor of computer science at Carnegie Mellon University. Luis does a test to see if students are cheating. He set up a website for a problem that was impossible to solve. If any student looked for the answer online, he was able to track them by their IP address. Forty out of two hundred students cheated. He found other tactics to get people to admit to cheating. Duolingo's mascot is green because the co-founder hates the color green. So, it was a joke on him. Luis' adviser at Carnegie Mellon was Manuel Blum, who is considered the person who discovered cryptography. Luis was trying to describe to him CAPTCHA. Manuel kept on saying that he didn't understand Luis. Months and months went by, and finally, Luis realized that Manuel was doing this because he wasn't being clear in his explanations. He said it was important in him understanding how to explain things. Luis said in Pittsburgh, a lot of people are there to stay, so you don't have the turnover you would in Silicon Valley. There is an advantage to that.

The Canvas Strategy

An age-old strategy is the use of apprentices, which clears the path for others. Ryan Holiday is a successful writer, who has held positions for a lot of famous companies such as American Apparel. He says that a lot of times people do not progress because they let their egos get in the way, as if they are better than the task being asked of them. But to become big, you have to start somewhere, and furthermore, you need to learn. There is a saying from Rome, *anteambulo*, which means clearing the path. If you can do this for someone above you, then you are going to succeed. Rather than thinking of it as slavery, think of it as a crucial learning period and a way to drive yourself forward. Another way of thinking of it is that you are handing a canvas to your boss to paint with. You are making their life easier, and you are making them look good. Ryan lists several ways to do this:

Maybe it's coming up with ideas to hand over to your boss.

Find people, thinkers, up-and-comers to introduce to each other. Cross wires to create new sparks.

Find what nobody else wants to do and do it.

Find inefficiencies and waste and redundancies. Identify leaks and patches to free up resources for new areas.

Produce more than everyone else and give your ideas away.

It's important to know that you can start this at any time, and there is no expiration date on it. The more you help others, the more of an advantage you have. The more you learn, the more favors you can ask for later.

Kevin Rose

Kevin is one of the best stock pickers in the entire world. He loves tea. He was one of Ferriss' first guests. They do a podcast together about random stuff called *The Random Show*. Ferriss once accidentally put his hand on Kevin's wife because she looked like his girlfriend. Kevin had some good advice on trolls. He asked Ferriss if he really respects someone that would troll. Also, would you respect someone with an infinite amount of time to do something like that? He hacked his high blood sugar by using acarbose.

Gut Investing

Kevin is one of the only successful investors that uses two methods. He's good at early stage tech and publicly traded stocks. He uses his gut, or an emotional response, to pick stocks. Ferriss says he uses a similar strategy. Kevin goes on to explain his technique. He explores a company by looking at his emotional response to it. Then he tries to think about the product and what emotional response it will have on the customers. He uses Twitter as an example. He invested in Twitter because he thought people would like the idea of being able to convey their message in short sentences. Also, the follower part of it was something he felt would be emotional for people. It would be a competition. He tries to see the product through the eyes of the people who will use it. This can be applied to larger industry trends as well. Kevin got to drive a Tesla when it came out, and he was shocked at how quiet it was. He didn't agree with virtual reality (VR) because it is too large and clunky for the user. He did predict augmented reality, though, such as Pokemon Go.

Neil Strauss

Neil is a writer. He has written several bestselling books, including *The Game* and *The Truth*. He thinks the key to being innovative is thinking and believing outside of the norms. That is where the new inventions lie. His book recommendation is *Life is Elsewhere* by Milan Kundera. Neil's best purchase of $100 or less is an app called Freedom. Freedom blocks everything on your computer for an allotted amount of time. He uses it to write and just write. He doesn't want to be distracted by researching something. He finds this to be the most efficient way to write. Use a placeholder, like TK, where a fact should go and revisit it later. He says to edit for you, edit for your fans, then edit for your haters. Neil thinks that writers block is like impotence. It's something you should be able to do but get flustered by performance anxiety. One of the best pieces of advice

Ferriss received for writing is to write two subpar pages a day. If you can do that at a minimum, something will come out eventually. Neil has interviewed many people. He says a key to it is being vulnerable yourself. That allows for the person you are interviewing to also be vulnerable. Three people Neil thinks are successful are Laird

Hamilton, Rick Rubin, and Gabby Reece. One of his favorite quotes is, "No matter what the situation may be, the right course of action is always compassion and love" (paraphrased from one of his teachers, Barbara McNally).

Mike Shinoda

Mike is a member of Linkin Park and has collaborated with many other famous artists. Mike talks about how getting misquoted can ruin someone's career. When giving interviews, Ferriss suggests that recording the phone call on your end is a good idea. If the person interviewing you doesn't agree to it, that should be a red flag. That way you can cover any possible misquotes. That is really what journalists are looking for, one quote. It's important to remember that everyone has their own agenda. Another thing to ask yourself is, what is the incentive? Is a media piece worth what they are asking of you? Sometimes it is not worth taking it. Royal Blood and Doomriders are two bands

Mike recommended to Ferriss. They are both fans of an artist named Hayao Miyazaki. Mike looks up to Rick Rubin as someone who is successful.

Justin Boreta

Justin is a founding member of The Glitch Mob. Some quotes he lives by are:

"Be the silence that listens."—Tara Brach

"Life should not be a journey to the grave with the intention of arriving safely in a pretty and well-preserved body, but rather to skid in broadside in a cloud of smoke, thoroughly used up, totally worn out, and loudly proclaiming 'Wow! What a Ride!'"—Hunter S. Thompson, *The Proud Highway: Saga of a Desperate Southern Gentleman, 1955–1967*

He has a reminder for Hunter S. Thompson's birthday on his calendar. It reminds him to not take life too seriously. Ferriss asks what Justin would take to a deserted island if he could choose one book, one album, and one luxury item. Justin said, *The Unbearable Lightness of Being*, Aphex Twin's *Selected Ambient Works,* and a Chemex. One of Justin's favorite artists is Boards of Canada. Some of the best advice he received was from his father who said, "Don't force it." Some of the worst advice Justin heard is that you constantly need to be inspired. He thinks you should show up and work, and that is where the opportunities will come from. If he could give his twenty-year-old self advice he would say, calm down. Three things or people he learned from in the past year are *Nautilus Magazine,* Brainpickings and Esther Perel. He recommends the podcast *Radiolab.* One of the best investments he ever made was a pair of monitors that he maxed out his credit card to buy after he was laid off from his job. He still has them to this day. In the morning, he does twenty minutes of transcendental meditation and a kettlebell workout. At night, he listens to Max Richter's *From Sleep.*

Scott Belsky

Scott is a venture partner at Benchmark and co-founded Behance. He thinks that people need to lose their plans to be able to find their way. Some of the failure he has experienced has made him successful. He describes how he had to scrap something that customers really appreciated in Behance to evolve into a product that more customers could appreciate. He thinks that sometimes you have to stop doing tasks you enjoy to nurture what is important. Scott thinks some of the worst advice is to look for patterns. That is not where innovation lies. The advice he would give to his thirty-year-old self is that your environment matters. Your strengths won't always flourish in every environment. If he could put something on a billboard, it would be that you shouldn't think of ideas, you should make them happen.

How to Earn Your Freedom

It is often thought that you need to be of a certain status to travel the world. Rolf Potts, who wrote *Vagabonding: An Uncommon Guide to the Art of Long-Term World Travel*, thinks differently. He thinks it's a matter of how you look at it. Ferriss describes his journey across the world and how little he had, but he made a point to travel at his own pace. They call this phenomenon vagabonding. Rolf delves into the idea. So many Americans think they need to live a materialistic life. This notion doesn't lend itself to the worth of experience. You don't need a lot of money to experience things. Exploring is a richness in itself. People often will buy fancy retreats or go to national landmarks for a short period of time. They don't get the full experience; they are just checking something off of their box. Rolf tells a story about two monks who wanted to travel the world but couldn't because of their vows. He said this is the way that most people live their lives. They don't take the chance to do something; they always talk about it. They save up all their money for hopes that they will do something later on not really knowing it they will. He also says that vagabonding is a way of constantly breaking habits, facing fears, exploring, and finding new areas of life that open your mind. Rolf says there is a difference between someone who has a ton of money and just decides to travel and someone who actually works for their travel. He thinks that work is a way to find yourself, to tie up the loose ends. It is a road to traveling. People who have a lot of money don't have this chance to explore or to dream about where they are going. Work makes it possible for travel to be a discovery, not an escape from who you are. Another tactic to make vagabonding work is to quit your job. There are ways to do this. You shouldn't look at it as an end but rather as a new beginning.

Peter Diamandis

Peter is the founder of XPRIZE Foundation, which is best known for private space flight prizes. He is the founder of Human Longevity and co-founder of Planetary Resources. Peter is a force of nature as described by many people. When he leaves a room, he often leaves people shaking their heads and thinking about what they are doing with their lives. He thinks that problems are gold mines, he doesn't see the negative side to them. When a lot of people doubt you, there are two scenarios. Either you are wrong or brilliant. He says if you are helping a billion people, you will make a lot of money. He got the idea of XPRIZE himself. He raised half a million dollars and then spent it all on the launch. Then for several years, he got turned down when he asked for money. He was close to giving up, but finally, someone funded the idea. Peter stretches and practices breathing exercises in the shower every morning. He goes over his three wins for the day before bed. Peter gave himself self-talk during his rough period. It included reminding himself of what his purpose was. He thinks that everyone should connect with their purpose. He recommends Tony Robbins' *Date with Destiny* program to find your purpose. There are other questions, like what you wanted to do when you were a child, that help you find your purpose. What would you do if you were given one billion dollars?

He also thinks you should get maximum exposure to environments where you can learn what you think about in the shower in the morning. He recommends the book *Start with Why* by Simon Sinek. There is a challenge to doing something ten times bigger than anyone else but with that comes ten times the reward. Peter says you should think about the questions or challenges the world faces and figure out a way to address them. He has several laws that he shares:

Law 2: When given a choice . . . take both.

Law 3: Multiple projects lead to multiple successes.

Law 6: When forced to compromise, ask for more

Law 7: If you can't win, change the rules.

Law 8: If you can't change the rules, then ignore them.

Law 11: "No" simply means begin again at one level higher.

Law 13: When in doubt: THINK.

Law 16: The faster you move, the slower time passes, the longer you live.

Law 17: The best way to predict the future is to create it yourself. (adopted from Alan Kay)

Law 19: You get what you incentivize.

Law 22: The day before something is a breakthrough, it's a crazy idea.

Law 26: If you can't measure it, you can't improve it."

Sophia Amoruso

Sophia created Nasty Girl, an online retail store with new and used clothing. She also created Girl Boss, which is a foundation to support women-owned businesses. She says that you should figure out what you are going to do, commit to it, and then figure out how you will do it. That is how she started Nasty Girl. A successful day for her is one in which she starts the day with exercise. When she hears the word successful, she wants people to realize that everyone can do the same things as the people they admire. It's just a matter of making the choice; they are not that much different from you. Her advice to her thirty-year-old self is that it doesn't become any easier.

B.J. Novak

BJ Novak was a writer for the hit show *The Office*. He has starred in many other movies. BJ thinks if you are using money as a term of contentment in your work, then you might be on the wrong path. BJ got Bob Saget to speak at an event of his while he was attending Harvard. He did this by pitching that he would give all of the money that was raised that evening to a charity. He said it's a tactic he has used several times to get a famous person in the room. He also said it's important to commit to a long-term goal before you start the process. When BJ first tried stand-up, he bombed so badly it took him three months to try again. If you look at it in baby steps, then climb from there because the short-term pain is more manageable. BJ didn't foresee the success *The Office* would have. Initially, they wanted to get a cult following. Steve Carrell gave feedback that BJ's jokes didn't seem authentic. Each season of *The Office* began with a period where anyone could shoot out an idea, and the more ridiculous, the better.

Part of BJ's creative process is getting in a good place to write. He takes his time in the morning, and he is more of a night owl. Every day he gets a coffee from Starbucks because he likes the consistency of caffeine. If he taught a comedy course, he would teach students to do parody. "Casablanca broke the form from its time period, and now it is the form." He suggests studying the following screenplays: *Pulp Fiction*, *Ferris Bueller*, *The Naked Gun*, and *Adaptation*. When he thinks of successful people, he thinks of Shakespeare. He thinks that Shakespeare made timeless things that moved generations of people. Some of his favorite books are *Daily Rituals* and *The Oxford Book of Aphorisms*. If BJ could give advice to his younger self, it would be to relax more. Some of his favorite documentaries are *Catfish*, *To Be and Have*, and *The Overnighters*.

How to Say "No" When It Matters Most

Ferriss describes how saying "no" can help you become more successful in the way you were meant to be. He says that if you are replaceable, then it is a sign that you are not where you truly should be. The easy place to be isn't always the best for you. You should go where your unique self stands out. Another question to ask yourself is, how often are saying "hell yeah" to things? Those are the things you should do. Everything else is not worth it. Ferriss asks, how much of your life are you managing versus making? An artist needs blocks of time to hone their craft. It you are busy managing your time, you won't have time to hone your craft. He thinks it is wise to ask, what excess in your life has become a curse and vice versa?

Then Ferriss wants people to question why they are doing something in the first place. This is telling you where you should go. Ferriss believes that it's tough to moderate certain behaviors. He invests a certain way because he can't handle the emotions of the other way. He works with it, even though a lot of people don't work like him. He thinks you should assess your weaknesses and work with those. Health should always be number one. Your days may be limited, and health is what allows you to live your life to the fullest. Ferriss will say no to meetings with friends or work if he hasn't had enough rest. Ferriss also asks, are you over correlated? For example, "Beware of anchoring to former high prices (e.g., "I'll sell when it gets back to X price per share . . .")." Ferriss says you can also retire and come back. If you want to do something different, quit and come back because it will always be there. People who take risks are methodical; it is wise to do your homework. If you are having a breakdown, you might be having a breakthrough. Think of the people that cause the most negativity in your life and scrap them. Write down what is holding you back from living your best life. Write down all the what ifs. Hopefully, that is enough to see that anything is possible.

Ferriss has met a lot of people living their fully realized dream lives.

PART 3: WISE

BJ Miller

BJ is a palliative care doctor and adviser to Zen Hospice. He has supervised over one thousand deaths. He is also a triple amputee from being electrocuted in college. When you are struggling with something, look up at the night sky. Ponder what is out there. It reminds you how you are part of the cosmos, and it puts your anxieties to rest. His favorite purchase of $100 or less is a bottle of pinot noir. He delights in things that are perishable. BJ tells a story of how one of his hospice patients designed a motorcycle for him. Ferriss concludes the story with the sentiment that you have no reason to not go after what you want.

BJ shares a story about being in the burn unit. He was very removed from the outside world. He had no window. Everything was very sterile. One day, a nurse brought him a snowball. It felt good on his burnt skin and he noticed how it turned to water. He noticed in that moment how everything changes and how beautiful it is to be part of this world. BJ thinks it is more important to empathetically listen than to offer advice. Ferriss agrees on this. If BJ had an introverted patient, he would put a Mark Rothco painting in front of them. His favorite documentary is *Grizzly Man* by Werner Herzog. He says that baking cookies with his patients in hospice care is one of his favorite activities. If he could give advice to his thirty-year-old self, he would say not to take things too seriously and be playful.

Maria Popova

Maria has written for several news outlets and founded BrainPickings. She has a tattoo on her arm that says, "what to focus on" with a bullseye that says in the middle "happiness." She put it on her arm so she would be forced to see it. Maria doesn't think you need to respond to people to decline their pitches. She thinks that if they didn't do their homework, you should not reward them. She doesn't do things out of guilt or prestige, which are opposites. Maria says no to a lot of speaking engagements because she doesn't want it to affect the quality of her writing. She speaks of a favorite quote of hers by Thoreau. He said, "The really efficient laborer will be found not to crowd his day with work but will saunter to his task surrounded by a wide halo of ease and leisure. There will be a wide margin for relaxation to his day. He is only earnest to secure the kernels of time and does not exaggerate the value of the husk."

Our culture wears working and getting no sleep as some sort of badge of honor. Maria says this is a failure of priorities. To drive this home, she recommends reading *On the Shortness of Life* by Seneca. Maria does most of her long form reading in the gym on the elliptical machine. When you are in doubt, Maria suggests doing what you like. You should write something you enjoy. It shows your readership. Maria gives a list of articles she suggests from BrainPickings:

"The Shortness of Life: Seneca on Busyness and the Art of Living Wide Rather Than Living Long"

"How to Find Your Purpose and Do What You Love"

"9 Learnings from 9 Years of Brain Pickings"

Anything about Alan Watts

The worst advice she has heard is follow your dreams. She said you have to walk through life and that can mean equal choices and chance. In there you find your purpose. She recommends three authors, Dani Shapiro, James Gleick, and Janna Levin. If she could make politicians read one book it would be *The Republic*.

Jocko Willink

Jocko is a Navy Seals Special Ops expert. He is a black belt in Brazilian jiu-jitsu. He has written bestselling books and started his own consulting company after his military stint. Jocko says his motto is "discipline equals freedom." Ferriss says that having absolute freedom can bring decision fatigue. If you have a daily workout, it creates scaffolding around your day. Jocko says that any sort of discipline will bring the things you want more of in your life. One of Jocko's favorite quotes is "Two is one and one is none." He thinks that it's important to have a backup plan for any sort of contingency. He also believes that in order to appreciate the light in life, you must see the darkness. He reads books about war veterans, and some of his favorite books are *If This is a Man* and *The Truce* by Primo Levi.

To an addict that was struggling to quit, Jocko said, "Be tougher." It's a decision to be tougher, you don't need to meditate on it, you just need to do it. Taking extreme ownership of your world is important. If you need something, it is your duty to explain it. Jocko uses an example of the military where when he was asked what was needed most of the time he said, "I'm good." That meant when he really needed something, it happened right away because his leadership knew he really needed it. He believes in early rising at 4:45 am. Part of this is his brain still thinking an enemy is somewhere, and he wants to be prepared. To indulge, Jocko drinks tea. He doesn't drink caffeine. It's an advantage not to need this. A good leader, or commander, will have humility. A leader needs to be open-minded and able to learn. Jocko also believes detachment is important. The ability to come into a complex situation and observe is important to understanding it.

Some of the men who died in Iraq on behalf of others are the people he considers heroes. He suggests for reading *About Face* by Colonel David H. Hackworth and *Blood Meridian* by Cormac McCarthy. One of his favorite documentaries is

Restrepo by Sebastian Junger. He listens to Black Flag and White Buffalo. He does not have a spirit animal.

Sebastian Junger

Sebastian is an award-winning journalist and made the documentary *Restrepo*. He believes that people need a group to belong to, whether it is good or bad. This is due to the history of men forming groups to protect their communities from predators. Being in action is better than waiting. He learned this watching soldiers who were warned of an attack. They were much calmer than they were when they were just waiting around in a dangerous place. Sebastian thinks there is an upside in disaster in that it brings people together and erases differences. He thinks truth is the point of journalism, and he also believes there is no writer's block in non-fiction writing. You need to do better research. Some of his advice to younger people was to not be afraid of failure and to not view the public as a threat. He also would be better at weighing possibilities versus committing to someone. He only types with one hand because that is how he learned.

Marc Goodman

Marc has a career in law enforcement and the FBI. He has built a career in the risk of technology. He says that Google and Facebook are surefire ways to put yourself at risk. If you are well-known, you should be careful and use pseudonyms because terrorists can find out your information and kidnap you. Personalized bioweapons are also a concern. Some people's information can be found online, which is why this is a risk. Two quotes he lives by are:

"The future is already here—it's just unevenly distributed."—William Gibson

"If we continue to develop our technology without wisdom or prudence, our servant may prove to be our executioner."—Omar N. Bradley

Some of the worst advice he has heard is that if you have nothing to hide, you have nothing to worry about online. Also, that we must sacrifice our privacy for the sake of security.

Samy Kamkar

Samy is one of the most innovative hackers. He hacked into MySpace, and his hacking has uncovered illicit mobile phone tracking. He is in the wise section because life isn't always about offense, it's also about defending your resources. For dating, he hacked into ways to find the best matches. One of those was shirtless pictures. Samy likes to code to AudioMolly.com and the Glitch Mob. His advice to his twenty-year-old self is to stop committing felonies.

Tools of a Hacker

In order to better understand your risk, Ferriss goes into ways you can protect yourself. First, put tape over your camera on your laptop and smartphone. People can spy on you through your camera and figure out when you will not be at home. On your computer, you can use BitLocker on Windows or FileVault on OS X. You'll Never Take Me Alive is a program that protects your data from being stolen in case your laptop or phone is stolen. Using different pins or passwords is important. You should never use the same password, and you should always use four to eight PINS on your phone. 1password or LastPass are tools for this. To detect malware, you can use NetLimiter on Windows or Little Snitch on OS X. Wireshark can be used for further analysis. BlockBlock will notify you if a program is installing itself on your computer without your permission. Plugging USB devices into your computer can be an issue.

Do not plug in anything you do not trust. It could have malware. Tor is a program you can install to cruise the internet anonymously. When you take a picture of yourself, it gives the GPS coordinates. You can fix this in your phone by going to settings, system preferences, etc. For instance, on iPhone 6: Settings → Privacy → Location Services. You can also use EXIF as an app. LinkLiar is a program that will help erase the data being compiled on locations you have been on your Mac. Some advice for images as well: in Chrome (similar tools exist in Firefox and Safari), you can go to View → Developer → Developer Tools, click on the Network tab, refresh the page, and see all content going across. You can then right click on any file, such as an image that the site wouldn't otherwise let you download and click Copy Link Address to get the direct URL. Google Reverse Image Search will help you understand where images on the web may have come from. Learning to program can't hurt either. Nighthawk and Wireshark are programs that can track all traffic on your computer's network.

General Stanley McChrystal & Chris Fussell

General Stanley is a four-star general. He is well known for his operations in Iraq. Chris is his right-hand man at the organization General Stanley formed. "The purpose of life is a purpose" is what General Stanley would put on a billboard. General Stanley, known as Stan, only has one meal per day at dinner. A lot of times people have a plan in mind, but they put on rose-colored glasses. Stan says make a red team to go over all of the shortcomings of your plan. It has to be people that aren't wedded to it.

When they hire people, they ask the question, "Everybody thinks you're great but…" and make them finish the sentence. It encourages people to level up on their shortcomings. It says a lot about their personality. When Chris thinks of someone successful, he thinks of his mentor. His mentor told him to look up to someone who is doing the job that you are doing for the better. Someone senior that you want to emulate, and someone younger than you doing the job you did but better than you did.

Stan has a morning workout routine at home, then he goes to the gym. He does all of this before work. He says that working out helps him because even if he has a bad day, he can say he had a good workout. To grow past fear, he says to push yourself past what you think is possible. He also says to put yourself in groups that share discomfort. You can learn a lot by other people's struggles. For people that don't have time to read, he suggests audiobooks. He listens to them when he gets ready in the morning. For a book that gives insight on combat, Chris recommends *Gates of Fire* by Steven Pressfield. *Once An Eagle* by Anton

Myrer is the book Stan Gifts the most. They suggested the documentary *The Battle of Algiers*.

Shay Carl

Shay's first video was about a manual laborer. He made his first YouTube video on the job. He now has over a billion followers. Shay invested in dietbet.com. It's a website where you place a bet with other players to lose weight. If you follow through, you win money, and if you don't, you lose. The secret to some of the best advice is to listen to clichés. Shay realized this as he has grown older. The answers are right in front of you. Learning from your future self is an exercise both Shay and Ferriss do. They ask what their future self would tell them and reflect. It changes the way you live your life. Some advice Shay had from his grandfather was that work will work when nothing else does. He uses these tools for shooting his YouTube material: Canon PowerShot G7 X camera and Final Cut Pro X. He thinks of his day as three acts and films it in thirds: morning, afternoon, and evening. He captures ten to fifteen minutes total, and he never shoots for more than two minutes at a time.

He says that vlogging can help him rise to a better mood. If you act happy, you will feel happy. When he thinks of successful, he thinks of people that have good relationships with their family. He talks about how getting influencers together with Maker Studios was powerful. He would put on a billboard that "You are going to die." It's a way to remember how short life is.

Will MacAskill

Will is an associate professor at Oxford University. He is the youngest person to have ever obtained tenure. He wrote *Doing Good Better* and has formed the 80,000-hour organization. He introduced Ferriss to Givewell.org, which tracks how effective non-profits are. Two of Will's role models are Peter Singer and Derek Parfit. He thinks that "follow your passion" is terrible advice. Jobs can be meaningful if they are engaging and help you grow. Also, they are meaningful if they contribute to the world in some way. For books, he suggests *Mindfulness* by Mark Williams and Danny Penman. This book is a friendly and accessible introduction to mindfulness meditation and includes an eight-week guided meditation course. Will completed this course, and it had a significant impact on his life. He also recommends *The Power of Persuasion* by Robert Levine. The ability to be convincing, sell ideas, and persuade other people is a meta-skill that transfers to many areas of your life. This book didn't become that popular, but it's the best book on persuasion that Will has found. It's much more in-depth than other options in the genre. His advice to his twenty-year-old self would be to think of how he wants to spend his 80,000 work hours.

The Dickens Process—What Are Your Beliefs Costing You?

One of the exercises at Tony Robbins' events is confronting what he calls the Dickens Process. You have to look at your past, present, and future beliefs and list what they have cost you and your loved ones. You have to see it, feel it, and hear the cost of what your beliefs have cost you. Ferriss said this process has changed his life to be a happier person.

Kevin Costner

Kevin is a famous actor and producer. He told a story of how on his first audition, his car broke down and he hitchhiked his way to the audition. He knew then what he wanted to do. Kevin said true freedom came for him when he stopped caring what other people thought he should do. As far as trying to tell a true story, he tries to frame it as "suppose this happened." This allows for the knowledge that unless you were there, you don't truly know what happened. He shared a conversation that he had with his father. His father spoke of how he just wanted to keep his job because it put food on the table. Kevin acknowledged that and thanked him.

Sam Harris

Sam has degrees in philosophy from Stanford and neuroscience from UCLA. He has written several books and has a podcast. Sam wakes up every morning and meditates to help calibrate himself. He has taken longer meditation retreats that he says make a significant difference in his meditation practice. He thinks that everyone should try psychedelics. He is aware of the possible consequences but thinks it is worth it. Sam believes that people with children have a healthier fear of things like artificial intelligence. He looks up at the sky to meditate, which is used in Dzogchen meditation.

Caroline Paul

Caroline is a published author, the first female firefighter, and was in the luge team for the Olympics. She thinks that secrets can be barriers to intimacy. She had this experience when she was younger. She didn't want to tell her father that she was gay. Her sister urged her to believe that secrets are a barrier to intimacy. Caroline told her father and he accepted it. Carlone mentions cooking for a fire squad and how someone pointed out the meal wasn't made with love. From then on, she has cooked with love. She said that pride can be a tool, it pushes her when she is scared. She doesn't want to make a mistake. *The Things They Carried* by Ferriss O'Brien is a book Caroline recommends. She talks about having fear. It can be useful to keep people safe, but it often isn't the most useful emotion. There is a visualization practice Caroline has where she lines up all of her emotions like bricks. She takes the least useful one and puts it aside. She used this when she was climbing up the Golden Gate Bridge at night. She also thinks fear is instilled in girls at an early age. Girls are more likely to be assisted with something seemingly dangerous than boys. She wants to change that paradigm and for girls to be taught the same courage as boys. Ferriss sees it as a skill to develop.

My Favorite Thought Exercise: Fear-Setting

The chapter starts out with a story about a lawyer named Hans. He goes paragliding one day and decides to quit his career as a lawyer. He had thought about quitting many times but always had excuses not to. He goes over his worst fears and none of them compare to a life he doesn't want to live. He then builds a dream life by having a tour company in Brazil. He never looks back. Ferriss goes into the same kind of story. He thinks about taking a year sabbatical from his business, but he is scared to. There are always excuses. Finally, he does it and finds out that none of his fears came true; his life was better. Ferriss has a list of things for people to do when considering following their dreams:

1. Define your worst fears in detail.
2. What steps could you take to avoid those fears coming to be?
3. What are the outcomes? What is the likelihood you could produce those outcomes?
4. If you lost your job today, what would you do to get things under financial control?
5. What are you putting off because of fear? Often the things we fear the most are the ones we need to do.

6. What would be the result if you don't do anything in five to ten years? One year?

7. What are you waiting for?

If you cannot answer this without resorting to the BS concept of "good timing," the answer is simple: you're afraid, just like the rest of the world. Measure the cost of inaction, realize the unlikelihood and repairability of most missteps, and develop the most important habit of those who excel and enjoy doing so: action.

Kevin Kelly

Kevin owns Wired Magazine and in his spare time runs an organization that is trying to name all the species in the world. He talks about a Buddhist practice where you meditate and walk. He applies that to life; when you do something, you should have 100 percent focus. He has a death countdown clock. He keeps it on his computer screen to remind himself how short life is. Kevin thinks you write to get ideas, not the opposite. He has had many tech predictions. He finds a lot of them by asking people what they think and flipping it. A lot of people wait to travel until they are older. Kevin did it when he was younger and had amazing experiences. When you are younger, he thinks you shouldn't focus so much on productivity but performance and fun. Middle age is for productivity. He gives away good ideas, and if they come back, he pursues them. He thinks being successful is defining it for yourself and living it. Kevin has reviewed a bunch of films on truefilm.com. The worst-case scenario is if you lost everything, maybe you'd have to sleep in a sleeping bag and eat oatmeal, which is something Kevin thinks about.

Is This What I So Feared?

Ferris delves into the idea that humans can live with less. He cites a passage from Seneca. Seneca talks about experimenting with living in poverty. Then, you will not be so scared if it happens. Ferriss has his own suggestions for doing this. He sleeps in a sleeping bag, only eats oatmeal or beans sometimes, drinks only water, uses the internet at the library, and utilizes couchsurfing.com in his own city. He said he almost always feels better after doing these things. We are often told to live with a lot of stuff. It is living with the least that often makes us the most happy.

Whitney Cummings

Whitney is a comedian and producer of *2 Broke Girls*. She says that for a while her life was all about work. She was paralyzed in the thought of being perfect. Then she began to rise out of it and realized that art imitates life. You have to have a life to make art. People-pleasing is a form of being an asshole, according to Whitney. She believes you take away the truth from them, and it is also saying they can't handle it. Whitney also practices saying "I love you" in her head before she talks with someone. She spent a lot of time judging people. That is a form of not dealing with your own monsters.

As a comic, she says all you need to do is break your own heart, and the audience will love you. Being vulnerable is what makes you tick. To train a new comic, she would get them on the stage. She says the first two years of being a comic is all about overcoming stage fright. To develop new material, she thinks of what pisses her off. She has tried equine therapy before. You choose a horse and have to lead it across a field with no reins. She says the entire process says everything about you. How you do things is who you are. She likes her coffee with homemade almond milk. She thinks Bill Burr is a genius, and she is a huge fan of Neil Gaiman. She gives a list of comics to look out for:

Sebastian Maniscalco (totally clean, no cursing, all performance)

Jerrod Carmichael

Natasha Leggero

Tig Notaro

Chris D'Elia

Neil Brennan (co-creator of *Chappelle's Show* with Dave Chappelle)

Bryan Callen

Bryan is a stand-up comic that performs all over the world. He says there are three things you cannot fake: sex, fighting, and comedy. He asks personal questions to come up with material. Bryan is one of the most well-read people that Ferriss knows. He recommends *Atlas Shrugged, On the Genealogy of Morality,* and *The Power of Myth.* One of his most gifted books is Ferriss' *Four Hour Body.* If he could say something at a commencement speech, he would tell people to go after what they fear.

Don't do it for wealth or an audience but do things because you love them. People doing impossible things is what makes the world a better place.

Alain de Botton

Alain is a philosopher. He has written many bestselling books. Alain says that when people are mean, there is often an underlying reason for it. You should take that into consideration. The definition of a person's success should include peace in it. The more you know what you want, the rest of the outside noise seems to fade away. He doesn't think you should expect other people to understand you. It's hard enough to understand oneself. Alain thinks that philosophers no longer teach us how to live and die, they succumb to academic pressures. He suggests philosophers like Plato and Seneca for practical living. His favorite documentary is the *Up* series.

Lazy: A Manifesto

This chapter is written by Ferriss Kreider who is a cartoonist and essayist. He says that people seem to always be busy. How often is the thing you are doing meaningful? This question is what he is trying to bring to light. He thinks that people should take the time to be with friends and family. He lives in a cabin with no internet and moves at a different pace. Ferriss does mention he has the means to do what he does. He says he is blessed because of this.

Cal Fussman

Cal is a *New York Times* bestselling author. Cal is known for giving top-profile people, like Clint Eastwood, interviews. When he was in his twenties, he worked for *Insider Sports*. The paper tanked, and he decided to buy a one-way ticket to Europe. He ended up traveling the world for ten years. He would ask random people if they knew how to make something, and they would end up inviting him to stay with them. Cal got to interview Mikhail Gorbachev because of his expertise in interviewing. He knows how to get to the heart of a story. He says he used to get anxiety when people were quiet during an interview. Now he knows to just sit, part of listening is just being present. A question that he often asks is, "What are the choices that you made that made you who you are?" Cal asked Harry Crews how he remembered everything with all the booze and drugs he took. Harry said, "the good shit sticks." If you want to write a book, Cal suggests reading *One Hundred Years of Solitude* by Gabriel Marquez. He would put "Listen" on a billboard.

Joshua Skenes

Joshua is a chef known for playing with fire. His restaurant has earned three Michelin stars. He was moving to a new space and all of his recipes were ruined in a flood. He decided to start over fresh. He didn't have a choice. That is still the premise today at his restaurant Saison.

Rick Rubin

Rick Rubin has produced music for artists like Johnny Cash, Adele, Jay Z, and many more. He has been listed as one of the most important producers in the last twenty years. Rick does saunas. He wears shorts and flip flops everywhere. If there is a dress code, he does not attend. Adele scrapped her first version of an album partly because of Rick's feedback. For healing, he uses an ice bath and sauna. He used to be a night owl, but his doctor recommended he go out in the sun for twenty minutes every morning, naked if possible. This changed Rick into a morning person. Rick thinks that the best kind of art divides people. Fifty percent of the people love it and 50 percent of the people hate it. That is how you know you are pushing boundaries.

If he could give his younger self advice, he would say, don't be so hard on yourself. Rick says that being hard on yourself is no help to others. Taking on something is like winning a war. You don't need to execute with perfection, you just need to realize people are interested in what you have to say. You have an audience, so don't kill yourself. When he needs to get artists unstuck, he makes really small tasks for them. For example, he will ask them to think of one word for a lyric. He says that a lot of his job is heart work. The head comes later. If you need inspiration, go to an art museum or study the greats. That is where inspiration can come from. He considers Don Wildman to be one of the most successful people he knows. He retired because he wanted to enjoy life and is an amazing athlete at seventy-two years old.

The Soundtrack of Excellence

Almost 80 percent of the people in this book meditate. The ones that don't have meditative practices. One of them is listening to music. Some listen to the same song over and over again. Most people pick two or three songs that uplift them. Ferriss goes into his routine when he has a deadline with writing. He will pick two or three albums and one or two movies and play them in the background as he works. He says it energizes him and he doesn't feel lonely.

Jack Dorsey

Jack is the CEO of Twitter and the CEO and founder of Square. If he could put something on a billboard, it would say "Breathe." A quote he lives by is "I know nothing." Some of the worst advice he hears is "Fail Fast." Something he believes that everyone else thinks is crazy is that "we are born with everything we need." He gifts *Leaves of Grass* by Walt Whitman and *The Old Man and the Sea* by Ernest Hemmingway. One of the best investments of time he has made is walking to work every morning. He thinks there are four themes in life: a love story between two people, a love story between three people, the struggle for power, and the journey.

Paulo Coelho

Paulo wrote the bestselling book *The Alchemist*. Initially, the book only sold nine hundred copies. It was only after another book of his became successful that *The Alchemist* took off. His daily routine for writing looks like procrastinating for hours. He says he procrastinates, then procrastinates more. Finally, he decides he will write for a half hour. When this happens, he cannot stop, and he often ends up writing for ten hours straight. He said that his mind has trouble stopping at night and he will take notes, but he never uses them. He simply lets what is important pour out when he writes. He thinks that you don't need to over describe. He likes to let the reader use their imagination. If Paulo feels stagnated in his process, he will sit and wait until he doesn't. If he cannot find inspiration, then he moves forward. He says having the discipline to finish something is the most important part. Ferriss suggests *Bird by Bird* by Anne Lamott for this kind of writing crisis. Paulo says he does not have a team of researchers for his books. Everything he writes comes from his heart. He thinks books are not here to show how intelligent you are, but to show your heart and soul.

Writing Prompts from Cheryl Strayed

Cheryl wrote the famous book *Wild*. She has written many other essays. Cheryl shares several of her writing prompts. Ferriss says these can be helpful, even if you aren't a writer, to get your thoughts out. Here are the prompts:

Write about a time when you realized you were mistaken.

Write about a lesson you learned the hard way.

Write about a time you were inappropriately dressed for the occasion.

Write about something you lost that you'll never get back.

Write about a time when you knew you'd done the right thing.

Write about something you don't remember.

Write about your darkest teacher.

Write about a memory of a physical injury.

Write about when you knew it was over.

Write about being loved.

Write about what you were really thinking.

Write about how you found your way back.

Write about the kindness of strangers.

Write about why you could not do it.

Write about why you did.

Ed Cooke

Ed is the CEO of memrise. He is an expert in memorization. He can memorize a pack of cards in a few minutes. He can memorize a one-thousand-digit number in an hour. One of his favorite authors is Goethe. One of Goethe's writing techniques was to lock himself in a hotel for three months and pretend that five of his best friends were there. He wrote a love story where things don't work out based on this concept. He would imagine the perspective of all of his friends. He was only twenty-five when he did this. The idea is that we don't need in-person mentors as much as we think. We can always imagine what a person would say. Ed had moments in high school where he would lose something. He said he remembers sitting in the bathroom feeling like a complete loser. Then, he would imagine the universe and the stars and realize what he looked like from that vantage point. He is a tiny spec in this vast place. It made him put things in perspective. Ferriss says it's close to the star therapy he talked about earlier. He recommends several books: *In Praise of Idleness and Other Essays* by Bertrand Russell, The *Joyous Cosmology* by Alan Watts, and *Maxims and Reflections* by Goethe.

Amanda Palmer

Amanda is part of the punk band *The Dresden Dolls*. She became famous by her Ted talk *The Art of Asking*. She explains how she got her name, Amanda Fucking Palmer. One of her enemies called her that, and a mutual friend started to call her that to her face. She took the name on, and now everybody refers to her as that. She said, "Take the pain and wear it as a shirt." For conflict resolution, she suggests saying less. On her success as a street performer, she said she would have a ten second love affair with everyone she encountered. Amanda does a basic yoga practice of vipassana meditation. She recommends the book *Dropping Ashes on the Buddha* by Zen Master Seung Sahn. She read it when she was twenty-four and it changed her life. She has given the book away to many of her friends and said it has had the same effect on them. Her advice is to aim narrow and own your own category. She tells the story of a stripper who didn't strip all the way naked. This stripper noticed that everyone else was doing it, so she wanted to do something different. All the other strippers would get a dollar tip. She had one person that gave her a $50 tip.

Eric Weinstein

Eric has a PhD in mathematical physics from Harvard. He was also a research fellow at Oxford. He has written about a variety of topics ranging from the metaphors of professional wrestling to his love for the movie *Kung-Fu Panda*. One thing he stresses is that mainstream fame brings with it more expectations, and it can be more limiting than underground fame. If you have a smaller, core group of people who hold you in high regard, it gives you more space to grow creatively. Eric talks a little bit about the dangers of consensus and how it is generally used as a tool to hide a greater truth. He says that he starts every presentation with the same Mark Twain quote: "Whenever you find yourself on the side of the majority, it's time to pause and reflect." Eric has a vast vocabulary and often finds himself trying to create new words to tweet out to his followers. One example is 'bigoteer': a person who accuses others of being bigoted for their own benefit. He talks about the fact that there are usually no consequences for those who falsely accuse others of bigotry or misconduct. Eric talks about the impossible and how his instinct is to find a way to work around it. He is very drawn to the stories of dissidents and their fight to not have their voices marginalized.

He mentions a book called *The Emperor of Scent*, which is about a renegade scientist friend of his whose ideas are routinely dismissed by the powerful people in his field. He speaks about the pioneers throughout history who at first are looked at as crazy, and then over time, their methods become commonplace. He talks about a member of a 1950s Japanese table tennis team who was seen as the worst player on his squad. He glued foam to each side of his bat, so his opponents could not tell which direction the ball was going to go based on the sound. It is an example of the power of ideas and how an idea like that can be seen more as a secret, or a truth that one person sees, and the rest of the world thinks is false. Eric speaks about his creative process and how bad language influences his ability to start creating. He talks about how when we say words that aren't polite, it sends our brains into an unprohibited space where creativity it allowed to flourish. He mentions that his creative process itself is aggressive, and when he is about to go into deep work, he utters a sequence of expletives that allow him to enter a mindset free of apprehension. He says he finds it easier to dive into deep work in the middle of the night when his phone is not going off, and there is no fear of missing out on any potential social interaction. He mentions that his younger self viewed psychedelics as brain melting, but in his later years, he was astounded by all the intellectuals he met who used hallucinogens to foster their creativity.

He asks why we never talk about teachers with teaching disabilities and only ever bring up students with learning disabilities. He then talks about how a lot of these students who are labeled 'learning disabled' are actually 'super learners' who simply learn in alternative ways that the average teacher can't provide. He ends by talking about his place in academics and how, even though he wanted to work in the sciences rather than the technological field, he realized he would be happiest in an 'expanding world' and not a 'contracting world,' where your mind is programmed to be on the defensive. His parting advice is for people to use uncommon methods to get better at things they think (or have been told) they are not good at.

Seth Rogen & Evan Goldberg

Seth Rogan is an actor, writer, director, and producer. His frequent collaborator, Evan Goldberg, is a director, writer, and producer. During a writer's meeting for the film *Neighbors 2*, a bunch of people were throwing out ideas while one person typed at a frantic pace. The word fuck was thrown around so frequently that Evan mentioned, "You can always de-fuck the script later." The lesson here is to let the ideas flow and self-edit later. They explain that usually the best material comes from writing what you know. They wrote *Superbad* together when they were teenagers. It's a movie about high school kids who aren't sexually active, written by real high school kids who really wish they were sexually active. Seth credits beginning stand-up comedy at an early age to talking about what you know.

He mentions he tried to imitate other comics such as Jerry Seinfeld. He was eventually pulled aside by a fellow comic and told, "You're the only person in here who can talk about trying to get a hand-job for the first time." Seth and Evan talk about what their long-time producer and collaborator Judd Apatow taught them. One important lesson in particular is that all characters have to have some sort of weakness. They are both marijuana enthusiasts and mention that they use certain strains for the creative process, particularly sativa-dominant ones. Their parting advice is to have blind belief in yourself, which they held onto when various people told them *Superbad* would never get made.

8 Tactics for Dealing with Haters

Ferriss talks about different ways to deal with haters, particularly those online whose vitriol knows no bounds. The first tactic is to gather a core group of diehard fans rather than trying to appease the people who don't get it. That will work itself out later. The second tactic is to expect a certain amount of people to respond negatively when you put yourself out there because that is simply how people work. You can never please everybody. Anticipate it and don't react impulsively. The third tactic involves ignoring the people who are just there to hate and get under your skin intentionally, while also acknowledging constructive criticism and not running away from it or treating it like most of the nameless and faceless trolls. Tactic four involves responding constructively, if you are going to respond in an attempt to diffuse the situation, with kindness and acknowledgment. Sometimes these people go from being your biggest haters to your biggest supporters. Tactic five: you can't reason someone out of something they didn't reason themselves into. Tactic six: "Trying to get everyone to like you is a sign of mediocrity. You'll avoid the tough decisions, and you'll avoid confronting the people who need to be confronted."—Colin Powell. Tactic seven: "If you want to improve, be content to be thought foolish and stupid."—Epictetus. To do anything interesting, you must accept and even find ways to enjoy criticism. Tactic eight: "Living well is the best revenge."—George Herbert. Robustness is when you focus more on the few who enjoy what you do; fragility is when you focus more on the people who don't enjoy what you do. Be robust!

Margaret Cho

Margaret Cho is a jack of all trades—comedian, actress, author, fashion designer, and singer-songwriter. She is known for her grand ability to shut down hecklers. She talks about responding to them with curiosity. Why does this person feel the urge to be a disruptive presence? The trick is to put them on the spot and keep asking them questions. Why are you here? Who are you with? Ask the person they're with, "Do they always do this?" When people attack her online, she usually will respond with a relatable quote from someone else. "Those who are offended easily should be offended more often"—Mae West.

Andrew Zimmern

Andrew Zimmern is an award-winning TV personality, chef, writer, and teacher. He hosts the show *Bizarre Foods* on The Travel Channel. Andrew, who was once a homeless heroin addict, has visited over 150 countries to promote new ways of creating and living with food. He stresses the importance of being yourself and not your 'inner actor.' He talks about going into a restaurant in Tokyo and being tempted to crack jokes about the English translation of the bar's name, which translated to 'morning erections.' A voice in his head told him not to do it and to instead be unassuming and respectful rather than go for a cheap gag. He then built up a reputation of being very respectful of different cultures while doing his show. When asked if he could choose only three herbs or spices to cook with for the next year, he chooses hot chilies, shallots, and lemon. He talks about their versatility and the many variations that can be done. He says when finding a good recipe, he looks for ones that are very detail-oriented because that lets you know the person has made that dish many times before to perfect it. He says the best investment he has made in life was shelving his restaurant career and working for free at local TV and radio stations to develop his media sensibility and begin his new career on television.

Rainn Wilson

Rainn Wilson is an award-winning actor, best known for playing Dwight on the TV show *The*

Office. He is involved in various charitable efforts, including an educational initiative in Haiti that empowers young women through the arts. He talks about being a thirty-year-old theatre actor in New York and driving a moving van to supplement his income. He didn't think he was capable of doing more than a few theatre gigs and a *Law & Order* appearance here and there. The best advice he says he would give his thirty-year-old self is to dream bigger and realize that he is capable of more than just the occasional TV guest spot. He talks about being in his own head a lot and how he finds ways to get out of it. Meditation, exercise, and being in nature are things that help. He says acting also helps. He can get out of his own head and into another characters. He mentions that his first Broadway performance was a total disaster. He tried very hard, but he was stiff and too much in his head. He sees that as a turning point to use his own personality to his advantage. Being sort of odd and a weirdo, he realized that he needed to bring that to whatever role he was taking on.

Naval Ravikant

Naval Ravikant is a CEO and investor. He has invested in more than one hundred companies, including Twitter and Uber. His family immigrated from India when he was nine, and he was raised in poverty by a single mother. His first name translates to "new man" in sanskrit. "If you want to be successful, surround yourself with people who are more successful than you are, but if you want to be happy, surround yourself with people who are less successful than you are." He talks about not associating with people who are always engaging in conflict. He mentions that you always have three options in life: change it, accept it, or leave it. He finds himself using the term 'accept' more often. He speaks about wanting to be a physicist when he was growing up and how science taught him the importance of honesty. In physics, there is no compromise, there is only the truth. The other way he learned about honesty comes from his days in New York, where he grew up around Russian mobsters. Being true to your word is held in very high regard amongst those circles. Ferriss and Naval both recount a story where they were at a dinner party, and Ferriss showed up in a flamboyant outfit. Naval couldn't help but utter, "Why are you dressed like a gay banker?" Naval sums this reaction up by saying, "The honesty thing is a core foundational value." Naval talks about how he told all of his co-workers in Silicon Valley that he was going to start his own company.

After a while, his co-workers were asking him what he was still doing there if he was starting his own company. He notes then that he was "literally embarrassed" into going forward with it. He says that 90 percent of his thoughts are fear-based, while the other 10 percent are based on desire. He talks about enlightenment and how it isn't impossible to feel a little bit enlightened every day rather than "sitting thirty years on a mountaintop." His best $100 or less purchase was a teppanyaki grill. He says that one important thing to know about food is it is often over prepared and over processed because it usually sits under a heat lamp forever. He says he doesn't have as many messages to send to the world as he does himself. One thing he always tells himself is, "Desire is a contract you make with yourself to be unhappy until you get what you want." He lists a number of different quotes that he tries to live by. They include:

"Be present above all else."

"Anger is a hot coal that you hold in your hand while waiting to throw it at someone else." (Buddhist saying)

"Praise specifically, criticize generally." (Warren Buffett)

"All greatness comes from suffering."

Ferriss then lists a selection of Naval's tweets that he feels are worthy of sharing.

They include:

"What you choose to work on, and who you choose to work with, are far more important than how hard you work."

"The guns aren't new. The violence isn't new. The connected cameras are new, and that changes everything."

Naval ends by talking about how his scientific background helps him realize that we are nothing compared to the grand scheme of things. "This universe has been around for probably ten billion years or more and will be around for tens of billions of years afterwards. So, your existence, my existence, is just infinitesimal." He says there is no excuse for being unhappy when you only have seventy years out of the fifty billion that is left.

Glenn Beck

Glenn Beck is a political commentator and radio host. His radio, TV, and digital platforms (including theblaze.com) have between thirty and fifty million visitors a month. Glenn talks about how people will accept you for who you are if you are unashamed in showing them. He talks about an early experience where a radio caller told him he thinks he is "Mr. Perfect" and can't accept flaws in anyone. Beck then went on an extended rant about all the bad things he has done in the past, exposing himself for who he was. He said it was a moment he thought would ruin his career but ended up making it. He realized then that all people really want out of you is authenticity. You should be willing to fail or succeed based on who you really are. An older lady he knew when he was younger told him "the righteous didn't suddenly become righteous. They just refused to go over the cliff with everybody else." It taught him to stick by his principles. He was given an uplifting bit of advice while studying at Yale in his thirties.

The professor Wayne Meeks told him to feel like he belonged and that he was good enough and smart enough to be there. He points this out as the first time someone gave him that confidence. He ends with a quote from Thomas Jefferson: "Question with boldness even the existence of a God; because, if there be one, he must more approve of the homage of reason, than that of blindfolded fear."

Tara Brach

Tara Brach has a PhD in clinical psychology and is a teacher of Buddhism. Ferriss speaks about reading Tara's book *Radical Acceptance* and having to stop about 20 percent of the way in so he could put into practice what he had already read. He talks about his favorite lesson on recognizing anger and other negative emotions. It's a way to face those feelings head on rather than hide from them. "Fighting emotions is like flailing in quicksand—it only makes things worse." Tara relays a story about the enlightenment of Buddha. The night before his enlightenment, he was in a battle with the Demon God Mara, who attacked him with doubt, anger, greed, and lust. Mara failed and left defeated on the morning of Buddha's enlightenment. Instead of ignoring Mara, Buddha acknowledged its presence by saying, "I see you, Mara." He would then invite him for tea and treat him as a guest. When negative emotions visit us, we can treat them like Mara. We acknowledge them and even open our hearts to them. It is important to treat yourself with understanding and compassion as you would any of your friends.

Sam Kass

Sam Kass is a chef who became the White House policy advisor for nutrition under President Obama. He was also the Obama family's private chef. His first rule is never serve anything you wouldn't eat. He talks about staying calm and prioritizing when he's in the kitchen. If you have a bunch of tickets and you try plowing through them as fast as possible, the quality will not be the same. Sam believes acidity is key. When you think it's ready, add another lemon. He says that eggs are the most difficult, and pro chefs usually test students by having them make an omelet. For the perfect scramble, he cracks the eggs directly onto the pan then stirs them. He takes them off right before he thinks they're done, as they harden sitting on the plate. He also talks of his love of soft-boiled eggs. He boils them for exactly five minutes, keeping the heat at a bubbling boil and not a "violent lava pit." He closes by saying that his true passion for food developed out of a desire to help people live healthy and productive lives. He says that passion is all about being open and curious and throwing yourself into what you love.

Edward Norton

Edward Norton is an actor, filmmaker, and activist. Edward talks about his appreciation of the director Toby Orenstein, who treated him respectfully and didn't look down on him when he was a young actor. She also stressed to him the importance of taking things seriously and not coasting through life. He talks about some of his favorite recent films, including three by the French filmmaker Jacques Audiard. Edward closes by telling a story he heard about a young Marlon Brando taking an acting class and how Brando was the only natural actor while the other students gave forced performances.

Richard Betts

Richard Betts is a wine expert. He served as the wine director at The Little Nell in Aspen from 2000 to 2008. He was originally planning on becoming a lawyer and was attending grad school when he went into a wine shop and had a transformative experience. He didn't know anything about wine; however, he recognized the label of one that he drank in Italy years earlier. When he tried it, it brought him right back to his days in Italy. He talks about how it didn't matter what kind of firm he was working in, he felt it was "all the same monopoly board' and became disenfranchised with the legal field. He mentions a few of his favorite underrated wines, specifically Grenache from Rusden. He stresses to "Try smelling with your mouth open, as you'll get more information." He has a tattoo that says, "Be Nice." He explains he got it as a note to self to be kind and thoughtful. He walked into the kitchen and asked the chef if he should ask for a job or go to culinary school first. The chef bluntly told him that it didn't matter. He would end up having to work an entry level potato peeling job regardless of if he went to school or not. So, he got peeling. He talks about "avoiding hotbeds for better access."

He went to work with a highly respected chef in Italy because no one else wanted to move there to work with him. He saw it as an opportunity to have better access to the chef and supercharge his learning by having more one-on-one experiences. His answer to the question "What do you think financially successful people who are generally unhappy have in common?" is "misplaced goals." He stresses that working for awards does not improve the quality of your work. He wishes he could tell his twenty-five-year-old self to "not be so fucking shy!" He admits he still has moments where he feels he is too subtle and not straightforward enough. He says that if he were a teacher, he would teach his students to love themselves because they can't love anyone else if they don't do that.

Mike Birbiglia

Mike Birbiglia is a writer and stand-up comic. Mike talks about how everyone is equal onstage, but offstage no one is equal. "Art is socialism, but life is capitalism." Mike pins note cards to his walls with quotes that inspire him to write. He likes getting feedback on his jokes over the phone because he feels that people are less honest in person and feel obligated to laugh in front of him. He likes writing early in the morning before his inhibitions kick in. He doesn't like consciously thinking about what he's putting on the page. He writes as if no one will ever see it, and that is the material that he uses the most. Mike mentions that he tries holding himself accountable, which can be tough. He found that he didn't have time for writing but somehow had the time to meet friends for lunch. He then wrote a note to himself that said, "Mike, you have a meeting with yourself!" which helped him focus on getting his writing done.

Mike sleepwalks and once almost died jumping out of a second story window. What would he put on a billboard in Times Square? A big sign that says, "none of these companies care about you." His best piece of advice is to ask people questions they aren't expecting, particularly if you're trying to talk to a celebrity or public figure. Mike and his wife met President Obama when Mike's wife was newly pregnant. They told him she was pregnant and told him "to not tell anybody." They asked Obama for parenting advice, and he responded at first with the usual "get a lot of sleep." He then went on a more in-depth diatribe where he told them baby poop doesn't smell bad when you first bring them home. Mike talks about it being the greatest moment of his life getting the president to say the word 'poo.' The advice he'd give his twenty-year-old self is to write everything down because it's all fleeting. He stresses to not bow to the "gatekeepers of show business" and to be your own gatekeeper.

The Jar of Awesome

Ferriss has a mason jar on his counter that says 'The Jar of Awesome' in glittery letters on it.

He writes down little notes about all the cool things that happen to him on any given day and puts them in the jar. This helps him on the days when he feels down. It reminds him about all the good things that have happened that he may have forgotten. He admits that his twenty-year-old self would be disgusted, but he says it's improved his quality of life tremendously. He keeps the jar in a spot where he can always see it. He tries to put a note in it every day, and if nothing particularly awesome happened that day, he writes "I didn't die today!"

Malcolm Gladwell

Malcolm Gladwell is a bestselling author and was named one of *Time* magazine's one hundred most influential people. One of his first rules for the morning is to eat a minimal amount. He loves lapsang black tea. Asked how he decides to start a chapter or book, he says there is never one good answer. He says he may try out several openings, but he never starts at the beginning because it makes things more complicated. He mentions the term *in medias res*, which literally means 'into the middle things' in Latin.

It refers to beginning a story in the middle or end of the narrative, not the beginning. His father, a mathematician, taught him to always ask questions, regardless of whether people think he comes off as dumb. Ask questions until you get it right. His role model in the speaking world is Niall Ferguson, who once gave him a birthday toast. He says the worst advice he hears being given out regularly is the advice given to students about college. He is very critical of the American college system and thinks everything relating to college falls under the category of bad advice.

Stephen J. Dubner

Stephen J. Dubner is an award-winning author, journalist, and radio and TV personality. Ferriss and Stephen talk about their mutual love of the book *Levels of the Game* by John McPhee. One quote Stephen tries to live by is, "Enough is as good as a feast." He says the only way to tackle a problem is to approach it with multiple ideas. He says that if you approach every problem with your moral compass, you're going to make mistakes.

Doing that excludes other possible solutions and limits your thinking. The worst advice he often hears is, "Write what you know," stating that he uses writing to learn more. When brainstorming, he likes coming up with a lot of ideas and then scrutinizes all of them. Whichever ones are unkillable are the ones he keeps going with. His advice to his younger self is "Don't be scared." He laments that there are a lot of things he didn't try that he now wishes he had. He cites the 'spotlight effect,' which is when you think everyone is looking at you and judging you.

Josh Waitzkin

Josh Waitzkin is an author and professional chess player. Josh talks about using empty space to nurture his creativity. He doesn't have social media and doesn't do interviews. He "minimizes input to maximize output." He talks about "learning the macro from the micro," which means that he puts forth a lot of effort on minimal details in order to maximize the bigger details. Josh talks about starting at the end rather than the beginning. When he learned chess, he wasn't taught a few moves to start out with. He was taught backwards, starting with an endgame scenario.

Ferriss and Josh talk about jiu-jitsu, something Josh is also an enthusiast of. Josh talks about his friend Marcelo Garcia, who he co-owns a jiu-jitsu academy with. Marcelo records himself training and giving away his technique, the rationale being that "if you study my game, you're entering my game." Josh talks about the three most difficult turns on a ski run, which he believes are the final three. He uses that as a tool when teaching in the financial world. If you end the day on a high note, that will carry over to the next day. One of Josh's favorite writers, Ernest Hemingway, would always end his day of writing mid-sentence so he knew where to pick up the next day.

Josh trains people to be able to "turn it off as quickly as you can turn it on." Right before a championship fight, his business partner Marcelo was napping on a bench while everyone around him was screaming with excitement. He was impressed at how relaxed Marcelo could be leading up to a fight. It inspired him to teach his students to be able to move smoothly between stress and relaxation. Josh mentions that the way to be able to 'turn it on' in big moments is something you teach yourself by 'turning it on' in all the little moments. He speaks of the importance of being able to take something you've learned in one area and be able to apply it to another. He recalls an experience when his young son couldn't get through the front door of their house. Josh told him to go around to the side door, which was open. He uses that experience as a teaching tool as well. If you reach an obstacle in life, try to 'go around' it and figure out another way. Josh talks about what he calls 'embracing your funk.' He mentions a successful friend of his who uses his eccentricities to his advantage. Josh believes genius and madness are both related, and that in order to work with someone who wants to be the best in their field, you have to understand the natural relationship between brilliance and eccentricity. He ends by talking about how it annoys him when people refer to rainy or stormy conditions as 'bad weather.' He feels that it makes us reliant on needing perfect conditions in order to be able to go outside and/or be productive. He teaches his son to embrace inclement weather. Now whenever it does rain, his son tells him, "Dad, it's such a beautiful rainy day".

Why You Need a "Deloading" Phase in Life

Ferriss talks about the importance of deloading, a term often used in sports. Deloading is a planned reduction in exercise in order to prepare the body for increased activity later on. Ferriss likes to deload as it relates to creativity and productivity. He likes to plan an extended period of work followed by an extended period of downtime in order to recharge. He cites a journal entry of his where he ponders these occasions. "If you want to be able to create or be anything lateral, bigger, better, or truly different, you need room to ask, 'What if?' without a conference call in fifteen minutes." He talks about how he schedules his week around periods or work and rest. He avoids using his laptop or any other screens on Sunday (other than his phone for maps and coordinating with friends). He feels deloading periods should be defended and taken just as seriously as business periods.

Brené Brown

Dr. Brené Brown is a research professor at the University of Houston's Graduate College of Social Work. Brené studies fear and courage and feels people have both of these feelings going on simultaneously all day. She talks about how we should "lean into discomfort" because our biggest societal issues (race, sex, etc.) are not going to be comfortable to fix. People who are willing to be uncomfortable are the bravest. She talks about her famous TED Talk, which is one of the most viewed TED talks online. She mentions that she let it all out, talking about her most personal issues, her breakdown, and the spiritual awakening she had afterwards. She left exhausted, thinking "I'll never do that again."

Little did she know, the video would end up having over thirty million views. It made her realize that if you she isn't a little nauseous after a talk, she didn't show up like she should have. When she does a talk, she likes to have the house lights on so she can see the audience's faces. Brené talks about the relationship between trust and vulnerability and how in order to trust anyone or anything, you have to be vulnerable. In her research, she finds the word 'success' or 'successful' to be dangerous. Her advice to her thirty-year-old self is it's okay to be afraid, but you don't have to be scary when you're scared.

Jason Silva

Jason SIlva is the host of *Brain Games* on the National Geographic channel. He says the best investment he made in life was in a series of videos he produced after he left Current TV in 2011. The videos became popular on Vimeo and attracted the attention of National Geographic. *Brain Games* followed soon after. Ferriss mentions that he is intrigued by the early versions of successes and is especially drawn to Jason's early work as it is quite rough around the edges. Jason mentions that the one thing that's become the most important to him is building his life around flow states. "The sense of being in the zone." Jason feels that if you are jaded, you might as well be dead. Being jaded kills your curiosity in life and essentially closes you off from deeper thought. One of his mentors suggested to him, "Be a skeptic, don't be a cynic." One quote Jason tries to live by is, "We are simultaneously gods and worms" by Abraham Maslow.

Jason's advice to his younger self is to not be so afraid. He realizes now a lot of the anxieties or fears he had growing up were unnecessary. Ferriss mentions that this is a common theme among his guests. It is always some form of "It's going to be alright."

Jon Favreau

Jon Favreau is an actor, producer, writer, and director. One of the first things Jon mentions before the interview starts recording is advice, he got from Glenn Close. "Don't go for funny. Go for truth, and you'll hit funny along the way." Jon is from the school of thought of writing what you know, because the truth is the easiest thing to both write and remember. Jon talks about how he uses cooking to bond with people, even total strangers. He feels cooking creates equal footing where you're all working toward the same goal. And at the end, you get to serve it together. Jon recommends the book *The Writer's Journey* by Christopher Vogler, which he used as a reference when writing his film *Swingers*. He credits video, and later DVD and digital platforms, for his films having a long-term impact. It showed him that a movie can be successful for years beyond how much money it initially grossed. He ends by talking about how meditation helped him conceive the film *Chef.* He was in the middle of meditating when it all came to him at once. He broke meditation and quickly wrote eight pages of material that he says ended up being all the heavy lifting of the film's conception.

Testing the "Impossible": 17 Questions that Changed My Life

Ferriss talks about how reality is "largely-negotiable." If you really ponder the limits of possibility, you realize that most limitations are a "fragile collection of socially reinforced rules." Ferriss lists seventeen different questions that dramatically changed his life. Question one is, "What if I did the opposite for forty-eight hours?" Ferriss talks about how in his first job out of college, he worked selling mass data storage to CEOs and CTOs. The job description consisted of cold-calling and cold-emailing all day. He failed miserably at first, then wondered what would happen if he did the opposite of most sales guys?

Call in the morning and evening instead of during the workday. Ask questions instead of giving pitches. He ended his emails with lines such as "I understand if you are too busy to reply" instead of "I look forward to your response." It worked immediately, and he was no longer failing at his job. Question two is, "What do I spend a silly amount of money on?" Ferriss realized at a certain point that he was spending way too much money on sports supplements (over $500 a month). He decided to invest in creating his own sports supplement at an affordable price. He begged his co-workers to prepay for one bottle and used the money to get the ball rolling on it. Question three is, "What would I do/have/be if I had ten million dollars?" The sports supplement BrainQUICKEN quickly became a huge success for Ferriss. However, he became consumed by work and was getting burnt out fast. His fiancé left him due to his workaholism. He realized then that maintaining that income came at the price of his health and sanity and that he could afford to give himself a break in order to be truly happy. He immediately took an overseas trip. Question four is, "What are the worst things that could happen?"

Ferriss feels this is the most important question, so it gets its own chapter. He then links back to page 463: "fear setting." Question five is, "If I could only work two hours per week, what would I do?" Ferriss explains that he decided to ask himself extreme questions in order to motivate himself. That's where the two-hour week idea came to mind. The real question is, "I know it's impossible, but with a gun to my head, how could I make it work?" It is the 80/20 principle, also known as Pareto's law: 80 percent of your desired outcomes are the result of 20 percent of your activities and inputs. It made him decide to focus on deepening relationships with his best customers and putting his more high-maintenance ones on autopilot. That process led to question six, "What if I let them make decisions up to $100, $500, or

$1,000?" Ferriss talks about how for a long time in his business, he was answering direct questions all the time from one of his fulfillment centers. He ultimately gave the people working under him the power to decide on decisions less than $100, so he wasn't answering every little question. He later increased the threshold to $500 and then $1,000. He then gradually let the reports go from weekly to monthly to quarterly. He mentions that people's IQ level seems to suddenly jump when you let them know you trust them. Question seven is, "What's the least crowded channel?" Ferriss talks about his apprehension before his book *The 4-Hour Work Week* was released. He wanted tips on how to market the book, and he decided that instead of sending out emails or making phone calls, he would ask people in person.

He felt that being one out of five people at an event asking someone for advice would be more successful than being one out of five hundred emails. He went to Las Vegas for the Consumer

Electronics Show and didn't even attend the event. He sat in a lounge nearby and struck up casual conversations with people who were in town for the show. He was adamant about not overtly-pitching, only bringing up his book if he was asked why he was there. He says that it worked surprisingly well. Question eight is, "What if I couldn't pitch my product directly?" Ferriss noticed during his book launch that the media doesn't really care about book launches, but they do care about stories. He realized people don't like to be sold products, and you need to find ways around selling your actual product. He focused on telling other stories on his blog and link people directly to his book-focused website. Question nine is, "What if I created my own real-world MBA?" He links back to page 250 for more details on that. Question ten is, "Do I need to make it back the way I lost it?" Ferriss talks about losing money on his home when he moved from San Diego to San Francisco. Rather than selling the home and taking a loss, he tried to recoup some money by renting. He found that to be a giant hassle itself and pondered why he was trying to make money the same way you lost it. He likens it to losing money on blackjack. If you lose $1,000, maybe it isn't the smartest decision to throw another thousand down to make it back. He sold the house and took the loss, relieving himself of the burden. It gave him the free mind space to make it back elsewhere.

Question eleven is, "What if I could only subtract to solve problems?" When Ferriss gives advice to start-up companies, instead of asking, "What can be done?" he likes to ask, "What can be simplified?" He talks about a start-up he worked for that didn't have enough money to redesign their website. As a test, they removed a bunch of clickable elements on the site to focus on the single most valuable click. Conversions immediately went up 21 percent. He has since rephrased this question as, "What should I put on my not-to-do list?" Question twelve is, "What might I put in place to allow me to go off the grid for four to eight weeks, with no phone or email?" Ferriss likes to ask this question in different variations to all entrepreneurs. He says because of the digital age, people go on vacation but are still glued to their laptops for business purposes. If you build up a business with people you trust to make decisions, you should be able to go away and not have to play catch up or fix everything when you return. Question thirteen is, "Am I hunting antelope or field mice?" This is a quote attributed to Newt Gingrich from the book *Buck Up, Suck Up, and Come Back When You Foul Up*. The book is about President Clinton's presidential campaign war room. In the book, Newt uses the analogy to refer to focusing on big things and not little ones. If a lion eats a field mouse, it uses more energy trying to catch the mouse than the energy it will get back from eating it. This is why a lion needs antelope. It's important to ask yourself at the end of the day, "Did I spend today chasing mice or antelope?"

Question fourteen is, "Could it be that everything is fine and complete as is?" Ferriss talks about doubling and tripling down on daily appreciation and present-state awareness. It's being thankful for the good things that do happen. He mentions that achievement is great, but it's really just a passing grade in life. To be truly happy, you have to want what you've already got.

Question fifteen is, "What would this look like if it were easy?" Ferriss says we sometimes overcomplicate things because we want to feel like we are trying our hardest, when in reality, the easy path is the best route. Question sixteen is, "How can I throw money at this problem? How can I 'waste' money to improve the quality of my life?" Ferriss heard this question from the strategic coach Dan Sullivan. What it boils down to is in the beginning, you are spending time trying to make money, and when you become successful, you should be spending money to earn time. Question seventeen is, "No hurry, no pause." Ferriss routinely writes 'no hurry, no pause' at the top of his journal entries. You don't need to spend all your time in life rushing to the finish line, panting, and red-faced. Simply putting one foot slowly in front of the other can get you the results you are after. Ferriss used to think the word luxury meant owning a lot of things. Now he sees luxury as feeling unrushed. He ends this chapter by stressing to us to look for simple solutions.

Jamie Foxx

Jamie Foxx is an actor, musician, and movie producer. He has a morning routine of doing pull-ups. He made up the name Jamie Foxx because, at his improv group, it was mostly men and a few females. He used the name Jamie Foxx so his name would be picked, and it was. Jamie doesn't believe in fear. He said nothing is on the other side of it, and it shouldn't prevent you from doing something. Jamie does a lot of impersonations. He thinks that either you are great at something or you don't exist. There are a lot of people out there trying to do things, so if you are not great, you will not stick out. His grandma stood up to a preacher who said being gay is bad. Jamie learned from that to always speak the truth. Ed Sheeran was nothing when he did Jamie's show. He insisted on coming, and he stood out since he was the only white person amongst a bunch of black musicians. Jamie was playing the piano with Ray Charles when he hit a wrong note. Ray said he was trying too hard, and he needed to take the time to find the right note. That resonated with Jamie.

Bryan Johnson

Bryan is the CEO of Kernel and the founder of the OS Fund and Braintree. He got a graffiti artist to do Gandalf the Grey and Harry Potter on the side of the house, pointing upwards with the word dream. One of his entrepreneurial gigs was selling credit card processing door to door. He was dead honest in his pitch. He said honesty is the best way to go. He was the top salesman. One question he asks himself is, "Is it an itch or a burn?" If it is an itch, it probably is not worth it. When Bryan was little, he lit a gasoline tank on fire. His mom rolled up right when he did it, and the fire was spreading. The fire was put out, but his mom said, "Bryan, you probably shouldn't do that again." He got a four-wheeler recently and said he gave his eleven- and nine-year-old boys advice on how to ride it by asking them to ride for five minutes, then come back and think about how they did it. He often asks what Shakleton would do as he was a huge influence on Bryan.

He thinks our existence is programmable. A quote Bryan lives by is, "Life is not waiting for the storm to pass, it's learning how to dance in the rain." There is a story he tells about a bunch of monkeys who go for a banana but keep getting cold rain on them. The monkeys then start pulling back a monkey who tries to go up the way that gets them sprayed with water. The moral of the lesson is that often freedom is a reality, but we make patterns that stop us from achieving it.

Brian Koppelman

Brian Koppelman is a writer, director, and producer. He's done movies like *Rounders* and the show *Billions*. Brian got the idea for *Rounders*. He was unhappy with his life, and he wanted to be in movies. He got his best friend and wife to help him. He worked on *Rounders* for two hours every morning before work. He and his best friend did this until the movie was finished. He said *The Artist's Way* by Julia Cameron changed his life. He writes three pages every day by hand. It's free form writing with no worries about the subject or mistakes. Brian said this has done wonders for his creativity. Three books and podcasts he recommends are: *Scripnotes, What Makes Sammy Run,* and *The War of Art.*

Some Practical Thoughts on Suicide

Ferriss had a speaking event and afterward, someone came up to him and asked for an autograph for his brother. Ferriss didn't think much of it and signed the guy's book. Later on, he was trying to leave, and the guy came up to him and asked him if he could speak with him. The guy said that Ferriss' book had a huge impact on his brother. Then, he mentioned that his brother had recently committed suicide. Ferriss was caught off guard and hugely impacted. The guy asked if Ferriss had ever spoken on this topic. Ferriss hadn't, but he promised he would.

The chapter then goes into Ferriss' own experience with suicide. He was struggling with his last year at Princeton. His thesis needed a lot of work. He decided to elongate the process, only to find his adviser telling him that taking longer didn't mean his thesis would be better. Ferriss took this really hard. He had made a lot of sacrifices to be at Princeton, and he felt an immense amount of pressure to succeed. Ferriss did take a year off, but his mental health started to deteriorate. He had trouble getting out of bed. He came across a book on suicide and decided that might be the best way to go. He checked out every book in the library on suicide for research.

His mom found out about the books because they sent a postcard to his parents' address when a book, he reserved became available. He said talking to her saved his life. He went on to finish his thesis and moved on with life in general. In retrospect, he sees how getting a bad grade at Princeton isn't the end of the world. But that is the point, people blow things out of proportion. He gives some suggestions for people struggling with suicidal ideations. One is the national suicide hotline: (800) 273-8255. Another is a website: suicidepreventionlifeline.org, which has a live chat. He said speaking with his mom was a huge turning point because he realized that suicide would hurt those he loved. This is something to think about before you take your life. He also says that committing suicide may not make things better, we do not know what lies after life. He also realized friends can help. One friend gave him a tip to make a pact with someone not to commit suicide. He says working out, expressing gratitude in the morning, and if you can't make yourself happy, making other people happy are good ideas.

Robert Rodriguez

Robert is a famous director, producer, and writer. He wrote his first screenplay, *El Mariachi*, while he was in college. It went on to win several awards. Robert made his first film around what he already had. Because of this, he only spent $7,000 on it. The film looked like it was made for $70,000. He won the Sundance award and changed the way movies were made in general. Constraints can be a good thing. Robert talks about how his film has snappy editing because the sound wasn't synched up. He would cut to a close-up of someone or something else to remedy the synching problem. Robert stresses to turn weaknesses into strengths. If you don't have money to do something, you can come up with a creative way to solve it. This can come off as a stylistic choice. He gives an example of how the building in *From Dusk Until Dawn* burnt down on the first scene.

Robert suggests to not follow the herd. If everyone else is submitting to film festivals, what can you do differently to stand out? Robert also thinks that failure is something you can learn from, and that is an important part of your process. *Four Rooms* was a failure. It gave Robert the idea to do *Spy Kids* and *Sin City*. He thinks that having a problem can help you build a solution that becomes a practice. He makes his own movie posters because he had to make one for a movie once. Because of that, he always makes his own posters. He takes notes at midnight to remember pieces of his wife and kids' lives. He thinks that life goes by quickly, and people forget a lot of key moments. Robert has studied great musicians and painters. The lesson he learned is that creativity is the most important thing to have. Then you need to get out of the way and just trust. Robert learned a lot from daily cartooning. Mostly that in order to make something happen on a blank page, you just have to start drawing. Something will come of it.

He points out as well that sometimes even the pros don't know if something will be good. There have been several scenes that were almost left out of famous movies because people weren't sure about them. These scenes ended up being epic to the audience. Robert says he does a lot of things because he lives a creative life. Then you can try a lot of different disciplines. He thinks creativity is one of the most important things to express in life. Robert got Frank Miller to sell him the rights to *Sin City* by asking him to make a short film and help him direct it. He said if he didn't like it, then he would drop the project. Frank did and Robert got the rights. He says that when he plays games with his kids, he bends the rules to win sometimes. His kids think this is funny. Robert suggests when pitching, start with the why. It makes a big difference and spells out the purpose for something rather than the less important details. Attitude is everything. If you think about it, you never need to be upset about anything. That is how Robert looks at life. It is all a matter of perspective about a situation that's meant to develop you.

"Good"

Ferriss gives the advice that for every problem he encounters, he replies with the word "good." The idea is that there is a silver lining behind every problem. For example, if you don't get the job you want, end it with the word "good." You have time to build more experience to build a better resume. This works for almost any challenge that comes along. Ferriss says to focus on the positive side of it and move forward. That is as good as life can get.

Sekou Andrews

Sekou is a poet and schoolteacher. He is a slam poet and has performed privately for many famous people. Ferriss leaves readers with a quote from him: "You must want to be a butterfly so badly; you are willing to give up being a caterpillar."

CONCLUSION

In conclusion, Ferriss says that he hopes people can get something from this book. Imagine these titans on your shoulders when you are going through a rough time. That's what he does with life. There are several one-liners that have stuck with him that he uses to deal with all the chaos in his life. In the end, he says life will make much more sense if you do some psychedelics.

THE TOP 25 EPISODES OF THE TIM FERRISS SHOW

"Jamie Foxx on Workout Routines, Success Habits, and Untold Hollywood Stories" (episode 124)

"Tony Robbins on Morning Routines, Peak Performance, and Mastering Money" (episode 37)

"The Scariest Navy SEAL Imaginable . . . and What He Taught Me" (episode 107)

"Tony Robbins—On Achievement Versus Fulfillment" (episode 178)

"Lessons from Geniuses, Billionaires, and Tinkerers" (episode 173)

"Tim Ferriss Interviews Arnold Schwarzenegger on Psychological Warfare (and Much More)" (episode 60)

"The Secrets of Gymnastic Strength Training" (episode 158)

"How Seth Godin Manages His Life—Rules, Principles, and Obsessions" (episode 138)

"Dom D'Agostino on Fasting, Ketosis, and the End of Cancer" (episode 117)

"Charles Poliquin on Strength Training, Shredding Body Fat, and Increasing Testosterone and Sex Drive" (episode 91)

"5 Morning Rituals that Help Me Win the Day" (episode 105)

"Shay Carl—From Manual Laborer to 2.3 Billion YouTube Views" (episode 170)

"Tony Robbins on Morning Routines, Peak Performance, and Mastering Money (Part 2)" (episode 38)

"The Science of Strength and Simplicity with Pavel Tsatsouline" (episode 55)

"Dissecting the Success of Malcolm Gladwell" (episode 168)

"Kevin Rose" (episode 1)

"How to 10x Your Results, One Tiny Tweak at a Time" (episode 144)

"The Importance of Being Dirty: Lessons from Mike Rowe" (episode 157)

"The Interview Master: Cal Fussman and the Power of Listening" (episode 145)

"The Man Who Studied 1,000 Deaths to Learn How to Live" (episode 153)

"Kevin Kelly—AI, Virtual Reality, and the Inevitable" (episode 164)

"Dom D'Agostino—The Power of the Ketogenic Diet" (episode 172)

"Tools and Tricks from the #30 Employee at Facebook" (episode 75)

"Marc Andreessen—Lessons, Predictions, and Recommendations from an Icon" (episode 163)

"Tara Brach on Meditation and Overcoming FOMO (Fear of Missing Out)" (episode 94)

MY RAPID-FIRE QUESTIONS

What is something you believe that other people think is insane?

What is the book (or books) you've given most as a gift?

What is your favorite documentary or movie?

What purchase of $100 or less has most positively impacted your life in the last six months?

What are your morning rituals? What do the first sixty minutes of your day look like?

What obsessions do you explore on the evenings or weekends?

What topic would you speak about if you were asked to give a TED talk on something outside of your main area of expertise?

What is the best or most worthwhile investment you've made? Could be an investment of money, time, energy, or other resources. How did you decide to make the investment?

Do you have a quote you live your life by or think of often?

What is the worst advice you see or hear being dispensed in your world?

If you could have one gigantic billboard anywhere with anything on it, what would it say?

What advice would you give to your twenty-, twenty-five-, or thirty-year-old self? And please place where you were at the time, and what you were doing.

How has a failure, or apparent failure, set you up for later success? Or, do you have a favorite failure of yours?

What is something really weird or unsettling that happens to you on a regular basis?

What have you changed your mind about in the last few years? Why?

What do you believe is true, even though you can't prove it?

Any ask or request for my audience? Last parting words?

THE MOST-GIFTED AND RECOMMENDED BOOKS OF ALL GUESTS

Tao Te Ching by Lao Tzu (5 mentions)

Atlas Shrugged by Ayn Rand (4)

Sapiens by Yuval Noah Harari (4)

Siddhartha by Hermann Hesse (4)

The 4-Hour Workweek by Tim Ferriss (4)

The Checklist Manifesto by Atul Gawande (4)

Dune by Frank Herbert (3)

Influence by Robert Cialdini (3)

Stumbling on Happiness by Daniel Gilbert (3)

Superintelligence by Nick Bostrom (3)

Surely, You're Joking, Mr. Feynman! by Richard P. Feynman (3)

The 4-Hour Body by Tim Ferriss (3)

The Bible (3)

The Hard Thing About Hard Things by Ben Horowitz (3)

The War of Art by Steven Pressfield (3)

Watchmen by Alan Moore (3)

Zero to One by Peter Thiel with Blake Masters (3)

NinjaReads

Thank you for reading our summary. If you learned something useful from this, please leave us a review.

We chase after the key points and analyze every chapter. You save time by not having to read all the unnecessary fluff that some books may have and absorb only the valuable & practical info you need.

Made in the USA
San Bernardino, CA
29 December 2019